# IS MORE

TANGIBLE AND TIMELESS WAYS
TO DIFFERENTIATE YOURSELF FROM
YOUR COMPETITORS

## HOWARD L. BROWN

AN INC.
ORIGINAL

# INSIGHTS FROM COLLEAGUES

"As a salesman himself, Howard always cared about the salesmen. He always believed that the more a salesman makes, the more the company makes. No matter what a customer asked for, Howard never said no. He believed 'make the sale, make the commitment, and then make it happen.' And he always found a way to make it happen."

**—BARRY GINSBERG,** Senior Business Consultant, HiTouch Business Services

"Howard makes a deal, shakes your hand, and the deal is done. He is the consummate salesman who would never say no to a customer."

**—GEORGE GOLDBERG,** Vice President, Business Development, HiTouch Business Services

"He's one of the best salespeople I've ever met. He built a good management team. He was loyal to them, and they were loyal to him, and that was a very big factor in his success. He's very community-minded, which is good for the community and good for business."

**—STEVEN GOLDMAN,** Attorney, Kramer Levin Naftalis & Frankel LLP

"Howard taught me to always surround myself with very strong leaders, so that I could focus on doing business. He believed that if you're not out selling and marketing your business, you've got problems. He always said, 'Bring on talent early. Continue to bring on talent.'"

**—GLENN POPOWITZ,** President, Direct Supplies Warehouse

"Howard's passion is obvious, and he's got great business sense. He's the best closer I've ever known. He taught me how to run a business, that you have to have a good cause and you have to believe in it. You have to see customers all the time, and you have to understand your customers."

**—MIKE PALMER,** COO, HiTouch Business Services

"Howard said, 'When the customer wants something, get it done. I don't care if you have to go to another stationer or a store and buy it, I'll reimburse you. Let's show them unbelievable service.' Whatever the customer wanted, that was the attitude."

**—CHARLES KAUFFMAN,** Vice President, Business Development, HiTouch Business Services

"Howard always surrounded himself with good people. He was always able to accomplish his goal of moving the business forward. If he saw that you had a good work ethic and you fit his model, then you were in. I think that's why he kept going back to the same people, because those were the people who were going to produce for him. If you had a good track record with him, he wanted you to work for him again. And people did, at two or three different companies."

—**MARYLOU MORGAN,** Vice President, Business Development, Regional VP, Sales Northeast, HiTouch Business Services, New York and New Jersey

"Howard taught me to look at a relationship with a client, or at the business as a whole, and not get lulled into thinking that things are going well just because sales are increasing. He believed you can't just take a top-level look; you have to look all the way down to every piece of your company and make sure they're all moving forward."

—**DEBBIE LAFFERTY JONES,** Senior Vice President, HiTouch Business Services

"Howard's mantra was, 'We're going to say yes and we're going to figure it out later.' That's why our company was different. That's why Howard has always been successful—because Howard is a little bit of a risk-taker."

—**JOHN FRISK,** President & CEO, HiTouch Business Services

"Howard had the ability to adjust as the industry adjusted and to back and nurture a relationship that maybe needed repairing from the past. Howard has been in the industry for forty years, but what's remarkable is how he had the ability to get into the new world of e-commerce. That was a brand-new phenomenon in our industry, yet he was able to adapt and really dive into the e-marketplaces. His commitment was the reason why we were so successful . . . From 2011 to 2017, we went from zero to $60 million in that business."

**—BUTCH JOHNSON,** Executive Vice President of Merchandising, HiTouch Business Services

"Howard was a rock, and that's probably the way he dealt with himself and his business issues. His personality and behavior didn't change one iota when things got very rough. He was able to look at and deal with his problems and just keep pushing ahead. His glass was half-full or three-quarters-full all the time. People who deal with stress well happen to be very successful. He's had many lives with his businesses. He bought and sold and bought and sold again, and that's pretty rare."

**—MARK CLASTER,** President of Carl Marks & Co.

"He is the ultimate optimist. He never accepted when people said, 'We may not get this business' or 'We might lose that piece of business.' He talked people into believing that they could get things accomplished. The most important things I learned from him are loyalty and honesty. He's very well respected, philanthropic, goes that extra effort and that extra mile. He is a pure mensch."

**–MICHAEL BROWN,** Howard's son and Vice Chairman, HiTouch Business Services

An Inc. Original
New York, New York
www.anincoriginal.com

Distributed by Greenleaf Book Group

For ordering information or special discounts for bulk purchases, please contact Greenleaf Book Group at PO Box 91869, Austin, TX 78709, 512.891.6100.

Design and composition by Greenleaf Book Group and Kim Lance
Cover design by Greenleaf Book Group and Kim Lance
Cover Images: BrianAJackson / Getty Images Plus Collection

Publisher's Cataloging-in-Publication data is available.

Print ISBN: 978-1-7334781-2-0

eBook ISBN: 978-1-7334781-3-7

Part of the Tree Neutral® program, which offsets the number of trees consumed in the production and printing of this book by taking proactive steps, such as planting trees in direct proportion to the number of trees used: www.treeneutral.com

TreeNeutral

Printed in the United States of America on acid-free paper

20 21 22 23 24 25    10 9 8 7 6 5 4 3 2 1

First Edition

*To my mother and my father—for the values they*
*taught me and the lessons my father shared with me that*
*helped further my career and allowed me to become successful*

*And to Nancy and our children and grandchildren,*
*who supported me and guided me to become successful in*
*family life, community life, and business.*

# CONTENTS

# INTRODUCTION

*I*N 2018, I SOLD MY THIRD COMPANY, HITOUCH Business Services, to the stationery giant Staples. I sold my second business, Allied Office Products, to Office Depot in 2006, and my first business, Summit, in 1987, to Buhrmann-Tetterode (BT), a Netherlands-based printing and fine papers company looking to expand into the U.S. office-products market. I believe my success is the result not only of hard work but two values that guided me: loyalty and reputation. These may seem like old-fashioned values today, but I believe they're still important—perhaps more so now than ever.

I'm writing this book to help younger entrepreneurs—regardless of their industry—to learn from my experiences and to achieve success. I've had fifty years of ups and downs, and I've learned hard lessons from both. I've bought more than forty businesses, which I integrated into the companies I was running at the time, then built and developed them, and eventually sold them to the big boys in my industry: Office Depot and Staples.

Many people may find it hard to believe that anyone (other than those two companies) could make a killing in the office-supply business, as the products we sold are so mundane: pens, paper, file folders, etc.

But I did. Three times.

I could have retired after the sale of each of my businesses, but I was only forty-two years old when I sold Summit, and I wasn't ready to hang it up. I was sixty-one when I sold Allied in 2006, and I still wasn't ready to retire. Even though I had a four-year restrictive covenant, I came back to the industry as soon as I was legally able. Even today, I'm fortunate to be in good health, and I'm up for the challenges of business, but I also realize it's time to enjoy my life—to travel, play golf, spend more time with my wife, my son and daughter, and my grandchildren. I still advise people on how to run and manage their businesses, and this book is part of that.

Over the next nine chapters, I'll describe some of my ideas about running a successful business, based on my own experiences. You'll also read comments from many of the people I worked with: friends, colleagues, family members, and business associates who can attest to many of the events and ideas I discuss.

Chapter 1 tells a little about my upbringing because I believe the habits and skills I learned during my formative years served me well in my career. My father was a successful businessman, and he taught me a lot—both directly, by inviting me to sit in on meetings and discussing his business practices and beliefs with me; and indirectly, because I watched and listened to him closely.

Chapters 2, 3, and 4 address the three tenets that I believe are most important to success in business: loyalty to your customers, loyalty to your employees, and loyalty to your vendors or manufacturers (i.e., the companies from whom you buy). I truly believe you reap what you sow in terms of loyalty with all three groups, and I witnessed that firsthand at all of my companies. I held on to my customers for decades. I had employees who worked for me for ten, twenty, even more than thirty years, who were happy to join me at a new company because we had worked so well together at previous companies. And I continued to buy from the same vendors, even when their competitors tried to woo my business, because I know loyalty pays off in so many ways. Chapters 5 and 6 describe how to grow a business by *constantly* looking for new products, new businesses, new services, new technologies, new markets, and any other new opportunities. Most companies can't compete on the strength of their products alone, unless you've created or invented something completely unique. (And if you have developed something brand new that's never been done before, you better make sure you have a patent on it because competitors will be nipping at your market as soon as they can!) Most companies can't compete on price, either, because there's only so low you can go before you're losing money.

In my businesses, my products were commodities; there's not much difference between the pens and paper, for example, that my companies sold and those sold by my rivals. So I couldn't compete on that basis. Therefore, I needed to find some other way to compete—and the way I did that was to offer amazing service. I also developed the "one-solution sell," so my customers could get almost anything they needed for their offices—from basic office supplies to coffee for their employees to furniture and more. I came up with other ideas for how to make their work easier, which benefited both of us. You need to do the same in your business, and the descriptions in these chapters of what I did should give you great ideas for what you can do to achieve your own success.

Chapter 7 tackles the bottom line. You need to know the basic financials of your business, in order to ensure that your company stays profitable. If you're not a numbers person, make sure you hire one—and make sure he or she is not only whip-smart but also dependable. In many of the forty companies I bought over the past fifty years, the owner was a terrific salesperson but a terrible numbers person—which is why those companies were failing and up for sale. I didn't want that to happen to my business, so I was always on top of our numbers, and I made sure I hired strong financial people as well.

Chapter 8 describes how to evaluate a business you're thinking of buying. I'll describe what I looked for, which essentially was synergy with my company. I'll discuss why I walked away from some companies, why I bought others, and how you can do the necessary due diligence to ensure that you're making the best acquisitions to grow your business.

Finally, Chapter 9 discusses how to determine when it's time to sell your business. Some people never sell; they want to maintain a "lifestyle business" until they simply shut it down or turn it over to the next generation. That decision wasn't what I wanted for myself, or what my family wanted, so I was always open to the idea of selling my businesses. More important, I knew when to sell, and this chapter describes how I made those decisions—for different reasons—at all three of my companies.

Throughout the book, I've tried to write about my business experiences not simply to tell what happened, but to show you—whether you currently have your own business or are hoping to start one—what you can learn from what I did and didn't do over the past fifty years. I've had a great career, and I hope the lessons in these pages help you to grow your business, too. Good luck!

# ONE

# START LEARNING ABOUT BUSINESS AS EARLY AS YOU CAN

*M*Y LIFE BEGAN IN FAIRLY MODEST SURROUNDINGS. My father Maurice, mother Eunice, younger sister Andrea, and I lived in Paterson, New Jersey until I was five years old, when my father moved us to Mansfield, Ohio to work for Mansfield Tire & Rubber Company. This was in 1950. He had three degrees—in accounting, finance, and law—though he never practiced in any of those fields. At heart, he was a salesman and an entrepreneur.

My parents didn't enjoy much of a social life in Mansfield, but my father made two great friends at his new job. Bill Leopold and Joe Kane were engineers who wanted to get into the up-and-coming plastics industry. My father told them if they could handle the inside of the business, he could handle the outside—meeting with customers and bankers. None of them had any money, but with the help of family and friends, they raised enough to start their business. In those days, it didn't take a lot. In 1952, we all moved back to Paterson, and my father and his partners started a company that extruded polyethylene film. This was the first of five plastics companies my father owned; each made a different type of plastic.

It may sound esoteric, but anyone who has seen *The Graduate* knows the iconic opening scene where Dustin Hoffman's character has just graduated from college and doesn't know what he wants to do with his life, and one of his parents' friends tells him, "There's a great future in plastics." The movie made light of it, but plastics were and are a great business. The plastic my father's first company made was converted into bags for the clothing and produce industries, and for a while, became the biggest extruder in the United States (although that didn't mean much in those days).

In addition to the company my father and his partners started in 1954, he bought another company in 1959, which developed heavier linear sheets of plastic used to make parts for automobiles. He also had another company that did injection molding, for plastic bottles for milk and other products. In 1960, the partners sold the original polyethylene company to Celanese Corporation of America. The money my father made from the sale dramatically changed our lives. We joined the local country club, where I met my future wife, Nancy Goldis (to whom I've been happily married for fifty-two years), and I met many people with whom I did business later.

In 1965, my father bought back the company he had sold to Celanese five years earlier. He had received a call from one of its customers, Sealed Air. The owners couldn't pay their bills, and my father was forced to take over their company. At that time, they were doing $12 million. Several months later, my father sold it to the brokerage firm Donaldson, Lufkin, & Jenrette; today, that company's sales are more than $3 billion.

My father sold all his companies in 1970, when he was only

fifty-four years old, and retired. One of his partners had died of an aneurysm at only thirty-five years old, so he had only one partner to persuade to sell. My father wasn't enjoying the business anymore because his companies had grown so big, he was spending most of his time in meetings, and that's not how he wanted to spend his days. Two of his companies were public, three were private, and he found five different buyers and sold them all at approximately the same time. He retired and thoroughly enjoyed the rest of his life, which continued for more than thirty years. He passed in 2002, at the age of eighty-seven.

## LOOK YOUR BEST WHEN MEETING CUSTOMERS—OR ANYONE

I learned so much about business—and life—from my father. He worked long hours—typically twelve-hour days—and when he got home at six thirty or seven o'clock, I sat with him almost every night to hear about his day and learn about his work. I started working for him during summers while I was in college, mostly in Oakland, New Jersey, at the warehouse of one of his plastics companies. From time to time, my father would invite me to come with him when he met customers. He had phenomenal relationships with them, and he wanted me to see how well they interacted. He also wanted me to accompany him when he went to look at companies he was considering buying, for me to observe some of the behind-the-scenes negotiations and due diligence, which I wouldn't otherwise have had an opportunity to learn.

I remember sitting in on one meeting with my father and his lawyer, when my father was considering buying a company. At all these meetings, I only listened. I wasn't participating, but I was paying close attention. After the meeting ended, my father reviewed what had happened, and let me ask him questions. Usually, the company had its own lawyers, but another time, my father's attorney was also representing the target company. I remember being quite outspoken. I told my father I thought his attorney had a conflict of interest because he was representing both sides. My father agreed but said in this situation, it had just worked out.

He always told me about those meetings in advance because he wanted me to dress differently than I typically did when I worked in the warehouse. He wanted me to wear a shirt, tie, and sport jacket. He believed in the importance of dressing professionally. It was one of the first things he taught me, and it served me well throughout my career.

In 1967, I graduated from Syracuse University and went to work full-time in one of my father's companies. I became a junior partner in that business. My father owned 25 percent of it, and he had given 10 percent to my mother, 10 percent to me, and 5 percent to my sister.

At first, I worked on the inside. I scheduled the equipment, did some customer service, and took orders from customers. After I learned enough about the business's operations, I went out and did some selling. The very first person I called on was a friend of my father. It was a big account, and since this was my first sales call, I went with the president of the company, Marvin Krakow, who handled it. The customer didn't really like Marvin, but he continued to do business with our company because of his friendship with my father.

I walked into our meeting wearing a suit and tie. Marvin was wearing a sport jacket and tie. When the customer came out to greet us, he said, "This is going to be a very short meeting because Marvin came dressed in a sport jacket; if he wants to talk about sports, I'm really not interested. But if you want to talk about busi-ness, I'll talk to you alone because you came properly dressed, in a suit."I took that to heart. From that day on, I always wore a suit and tie when meeting with customers. And I insisted that my sales-men at least wear a jacket and tie. At first, they were all men, but as my businesses grew, more women joined the sales force, and I wanted them to look professional as well. I understood that some people didn't own enough suits to wear one every day, so if they wanted to wear a sports jacket or a navy blazer, that was fine with me, but I wanted the men to wear a tie, and I wanted everyone who met with customers to look professional. I believe that how you look is how you represent your company. Even today, when casual dress is accepted and has become the norm in many industries, many people are still impressed by a well-dressed businessperson. That may seem old-fashioned, but I never go to any business meet-ing unless I'm wearing a suit.

## PUT YOURSELF IN THE OTHER PERSON'S SHOES

Another thing I learned from my father was to try to put myself in the other person's shoes. He taught me that there will always be "bottom fishers"—people who want to get the best deal they can, any way they can, and that's not a good way to negotiate deals. It generates ill will between parties. He believed that negotiations (and business in general) didn't need to be adversarial, where one person wins and the other loses. Instead, try to ascertain what the other person *really* wants or needs from the deal, which may be different from what that person *says* he or she wants or needs.

For example, I remember him telling me about a situation when a stubborn negotiator gave him an ultimatum, saying, "That's my price; take it or leave it." My father thought it was still a good deal, so he was willing to pay the higher price. He believed that if a business was worth $1 million, for example, it was probably also worth $1.2 million. However, one of his partners thought my father was overpaying, and my father acceded to his partners. He lost the deal.

Later, after that business sold to someone else, my father's partners realized that even the higher price would have been a good deal. My father knew it had been a mistake to walk away, but he did what his partners wanted to do. He didn't believe in overpaying, but he also didn't believe in squeezing every last dollar out of a deal. As it turned out, that was the last time my father ever listened to his partners when they did deals, and his partners never interfered again. Like many partnerships, they worked together best when each partner did what he knew how to do and didn't interfere with the other partners' areas of expertise.

The real lesson my father wanted me to learn from that experience was that if you want to make a deal, find out what's most important to the other person. Understand what that person is looking for, and try to back into that situation your own way. That's good advice in every interaction and relationship with another person, and it helped me enormously in business. If someone tells you they want $2.5 million for their business, but also reveals that they need $1.5 million to retire, then you know that the real number is somewhere between $1.5 and $2.5 million. If you let a person talk, you will usually find out what the real number is, or what's really important to them in making this deal. You might offer $1.7 million, and if they push you to $1.75 million, you still didn't pay the full $2.5 million they originally asked, but they got more than they wanted, and you paid less.

## SURROUND YOURSELF WITH GOOD PEOPLE

My father also taught me the importance of working with good people. He taught me to surround myself with them and then to take care of your team. Once, he invited his accountant, his lawyer, and his electrician to be partners in the company he bought back from Celanese in 1965. All three of them were with him from the very beginning. They invested because they knew what a good businessman my father was, and they saw the benefits, financial and otherwise, of that investment.

He also believed in rewarding his people when they exceeded expectations. In addition to end-of-year bonuses and pay increases, if someone sold an especially large order, he gave what he called a "Be My Guest" dinner as a reward to that person and his or her family. My father wanted to do something for an employee's entire family because he knew that if the spouse and children were included, they would also be supportive when we needed our people to work long hours. He had a summertime picnic for employees and their entire families, with prizes for the children. He believed a happy family made a happy employee.

I also took to heart that advice about employees, and it became one of the fundamental tenets of the way I do business. Once you find good employees, don't let them slip away. When you move on, try to take the best people with you. I've had three very successful entities in my 46-year career, and many of my employees have moved with me from company to company. Even when I couldn't work in the industry for several years because of restrictive covenants following the sale of each, many of my employees worked elsewhere during those years then quickly joined me in my next venture. They were loyal to me because I was loyal to them, and I helped them whenever I could.

During his retirement, my father was still interested in business. I talked to him every day, calling him on my way home from the office, and he always asked me, "How is *gescheft*?" (*Gescheft* is Yiddish for *business*.) I always valued his input; he was my mentor. I even brought him with me occasionally when I was looking at companies I was thinking of buying.

He advised other people, too, on business issues. I do the same thing, today. I've advised people—especially young people, starting out—on how to handle certain situations, and they're eager to learn. I realize some people "retire" and set themselves up as fee-based consultants, but I'm not interested in doing that, at least not yet. If I can help someone by providing insight from my years of experience, I'm happy to do so. My father helped me, and I've always tried to help others.

The next chapter takes a closer look at the importance of being loyal to your customers.

## *START LEARNING ABOUT BUSINESS AS EARLY AS YOU CAN:*

1. ***Dress for success.*** Looking professional can open up a lot of doors, so don't squander this opportunity. Dress as well as your budget will allow.

2. ***Put yourself in the other person's shoes.*** In any business deal or negotiation, try to figure out what's important to the other person. That usually enables you to negotiate a deal that's still appealing to them but at a lower price for you.

3. ***Hire good people, and take care of them.*** It's much easier to be successful in business when you have long-lasting relationships, built on mutual trust and loyalty.

# TWO

# BUILD RELATIONSHIPS WITH YOUR CUSTOMERS

Loyalty to customers is especially critical in a commodities business, like office supplies (and other businesses, too). People and companies can buy pens and paper from anyone. It would be ridiculous for me to tell customers how much better my Bic pen is than the Bic pen my competitor is selling.

## TALK PASSIONATELY ABOUT YOUR BUSINESS

However, what I *can* talk about is my pricing. I can talk about my service. I can talk about the breadth of my product line, which bene-fits customers because they can do one-stop shopping with me, which they often can't do with my competitors. I tell them about not only the office supplies we sell but also the promotional products (t-shirts, baseball caps, pens, calendars, and anything with a customer's name and logo on it). I tell them about the printing services we can offer them. I tell them about the coffee and beverage services we can provide—which, by the way, opened up an entirely new, huge market for us and made customers' purchasing so much easier. And finally, I tell them about the office furniture and janitorial supplies we sell.

There's nothing exciting about office supplies or janitorial products. In any business that deals with commodity products, the only way to differentiate your company is by creating added value and by developing a relationship with your customers. You need to ensure that customers want to buy from *you,* so they'll continue to buy from your company.

To develop these relationships, you first need great salespeople. I firmly believe that the company owner is the best salesperson for his or her products. Even though I bought an existing business, and forty other businesses over the next forty-five years, I *built* businesses. My companies were my babies, and like the way parents brag about their children, when I talked about my business, people could see the passion I had for it. The passion isn't about the products; it's about how the product can serve the customer. When customers saw my passion, they were impressed and wanted to do business with my companies.

## SELL TO EVERYONE YOU MEET

I spent about 50 percent of my time selling, though it feels as if I was selling every waking hour of every day because it's second nature to me. Eventually, I asked everyone I met where they bought their office supplies. I learned this from my father, who was a terrific salesman. Even though he was educated in accounting, finance, and law, he didn't fit the stereotype of those professions. He was a people person. From an early age, I went with him on sales calls and watched the way he talked and interacted with his customers, and I learned a lot about how to do business from him.

Of course, I wasn't the only salesperson for my companies. You can't be; you need a great team, and I had some terrific salespeople. I found that the best way to get a foot in the door was to start at the top, the C-suite. The owner of a private company or the CEO of a public company is more likely to do business with another company's owner than with a salesperson, no matter how talented that salesperson may be. I opened the door, then I turned over the accounts to my salespeople  while still maintaining a relationship with my initial contact.

Most people don't care where they buy their office supplies. The products are too mundane. Whenever I met someone new, I always found a way to ask who that person bought from. Then I asked to take a look at their bills. I'd tell people straight out, "I'd love to come in and see if I can save you money." Who doesn't want to save money? Everyone wants to save money. I don't remember many people saying, "I don't need to save money in my business."

Several of my early customers came through social connections I made at my country club. I'd been a member since I was fifteen, when my parents joined. Our club was also the source of my initial business, when I bought into Summit Office Supply because another club member wanted to sell his share in Summit and retire. I played golf every weekend, and the people I played with always asked me, "What do you do for a living?" When I told them I was in the office supply business, they encouraged me to call them at work. This was an easy way in, and the people I was playing golf with typically owned their businesses, which meant I was selling in at the top.

You don't need to be a member of a country club to find customers;

everyone has social connections. Contact people you know from your neighborhood, your schools, your children's schools, your alma mater, your church, synagogue, or any other religious organization you belong to. I can't emphasize enough the importance of networking. In sales, we ask everyone we know to introduce us to their friends and associates because every business buys what we sell.

I also found new customers when I did business with other companies. For example, I made investments with a few local start-up banks. I said something like this to the CEO: "If I make an investment in your bank, why shouldn't I be selling you office supplies at all your branches?" I also went one step further, offering to warehouse their proprietary supplies—anything that was printed with their name and logo. I said, "You're delivering envelopes and other supplies to all your branches when they run out. We can deliver everything for you, so you don't need to worry about that anymore."

They were always happy to have me come in and talk further. The bank president or CEO would then introduce us to the bank's purchasing people by saying something like, "Mr. Brown is a shareholder of the bank. He tells me he can save us a lot of money. We don't have to carry the inventory for lollipops, and pens, or any of our other promotional products—all the items we give away when people open up a new account. His company is going to deliver our office supplies, coffee, and beverages. He will also handle furniture and everything else. I want you to sit down with him and review all our bills from the vendors we're currently buying from, and he'll tell us how much he can save us." When the bank president or CEO has that conversation, the purchasing agent always listens.

That's the main reason I want to connect with CEOs and business owners, because I talk passionately about my business, and I make the CEO or owner feel that passion. Many business owners have said to my face, "I wish you worked for me. I wish my people had that kind of passion." They're happy to let me look at their bills from other vendors, to see where I can save them money, whereas purchasing agents are inclined to say, "We don't like to share pricing information," and if we don't know what they're paying, it's obviously more difficult to offer them a lower price.

The people I met through philanthropic connections were another source of potential customers. My wife and I started our involvement by giving to UJA (United Jewish Appeal); over the years, we've expanded into many other areas. When my daughter was diagnosed with Crohn's disease, we got involved with doctors in New York City, and my wife joined the Crohn's and Colitis Foundation, later becoming the president of the New York chapter. About twenty-five years ago, she started a luncheon to raise money for it. The first year, about sixty women attended and contributed $100,000. For each of the past ten years, a thousand women attended, and she raised approximately $2 million a year.

Nancy is now on the board of four or five charities, and we donate to many more. In fact, I sometimes joke that I keep working so I can support our charities. However, that's not a bad reason to work. I've met many people at social functions or charitable dinners who have become customers of my business.

## FIND SELLING OPPORTUNITIES BY BEING OBSERVANT

Every time I walk into an office, I look around. You need to be observant in order to find sales opportunities. For example, I recently had a meeting with Staples (which bought my third company, HiTouch

Business Services), at the offices of one of their law firms. On the way in, I noticed that the paper stacked next to the copy machine wasn't a Staples product. When I sat down with the execs, I mentioned this, and they turned to their lawyers and asked, "Where do you buy your paper?" Of course, the lawyers didn't know, so they called their purchasing manager, who said matter-of-factly that he bought the firm's office supplies from one of Staples' competitors. As he explained, "Nobody told me I needed to buy our paper from Staples."

Obviously, that changed immediately, and by the time I left the office, Staples had that account.

That was important to me because I believe in reciprocal relationships. If I'm doing business with you, I'd like you to be doing business with me. Believe it or not, most people don't think this way. But if I hire a lawyer or an accountant, or anyone in business who uses office supplies, I want him or her to buy office supplies from me. After all, the lawyer has to buy them somewhere, so why not from one of his or her clients? I also ask my business contacts to introduce me to their business contacts.

My lawyer is on the board of a major bank, so I asked him to set up a meeting with the bank's CEO. As it happened, they were buying their office supplies from Office Depot, but I persuaded them to buy from us. It took a year to convert all the business, but eventually, we had the bank's entire account, including a major furniture order when the bank consolidated several offices in New York City.

Admittedly, there have been situations where someone has another client who competes with my business in some product area, but even then, I'll ask if I can handle the part of the business that my competitor isn't currently handling.

When I started selling office furniture (a natural extension of office supplies, but one that wasn't obvious to most companies when I started in this industry), I approached all my customers to see if they needed anything. One of my clients—another lawyer—was remodeling his office. I asked for his furniture business. He told me he had another, long-standing client who specialized in furniture, and he had been buying from that client for years. I understood completely, and that customer continued to buy paper and other office supplies from me while buying his furniture from his other client; there was no way I could make inroads in his furniture business as long as that other company was his client. That happens all the time; still, it never hurts to ask for new business.

I had the same experience with one of my hospital clients. My company sold the hospital about $3 million a year in office products, everything except printing services. The hospital had been buying these from another company for years, and it was very happy with the service it was getting. I knew I could save the hospital 15 to 20 percent on its printing, but there was no point trying to continue the conversation and persuade the purchasing manager because he told me the other company had been very loyal and reliable to the hospital for many years. I know when to push a little bit and when to back off. Whenever I knew I wasn't going to get the business, I always politely withdrew, to maintain the great relationship I had with my customers. But I asked about other products, like janitorial & sanitation supplies, and they switched $1 million of that business to us.

My salespeople did the same thing. They respected whatever boundaries their customers set, but they also tried to nibble at new business whenever they could. If one of their customers complained about another company they were buying from, or even if a customer simply mentioned in passing that something he or she had ordered from another company had been delivered late, my salesmen knew it was their opportunity to offer to take over that business by saying, "If you give me an opportunity, I'll have it delivered tomorrow." To make those offers, they needed to be in front of their customers regularly. They needed to know what their customers' problems were, so they could offer a solution. To be effective, they needed to visit their customers often.

## MAINTAIN CUSTOMER RELATIONSHIPS BY DELIVERING OUTSTANDING SERVICE

I continue to be amazed at how many businesses think that once they have a customer, they have them for life, and they don't need to do any follow-up to maintain that relationship. It's not the case at all. I believe you need to visit your customers regularly, and you need to be selling all the time. That's the way I've managed all my businesses, and that's one of the reasons I think I've been so successful. It's the relationship with the customer that's important, and at Summit, Allied, and HiTouch, we worked hard to maintain those relationships.

It doesn't matter what business you're in. Whether you're selling a product or a service, there's always an opportunity to ask someone if they're happy with the product or service they're getting. If you're selling a service, for example, ask "Are you happy with the time it takes your current vendor to deliver?" If the answer is no, and if you're confident that you can deliver faster, that's your opening. You need to know what's most important to potential customers, and then you need to sell to your strengths. Get them talking, and find out what their frustrations are. If one of your strengths is speed, that's what you should emphasize because that's important to a lot of people and a lot of businesses. Try to find out what your competition's weaknesses are, and if those same factors are your strengths, you have a better chance of taking away that business from your competition.

I was meeting with another lawyer when I noticed his firm bought paper from W.B. Mason, one of our main competitors. (The company name is on the wrapper around every ream and on every box, so it didn't require any detective work on my part.) During a break in our meeting, I commented, "I see you buy your paper from W.B. Mason; do you know what you pay per carton?" I wasn't surprised when he said, "I'm a senior partner at this firm; I have no idea. Our office manager takes care of all the buying. But we have twenty lawyers here, and we use a lot of paper." I asked him if he would mind finding out what the firm was paying, so he picked up the phone and called his office manager.

He said, "We pay thirty-seven fifty a carton; is that a good price?" I told him, "It's not a bad price, but I'll charge you thirty-two fifty per carton." I didn't even need to calculate the savings for him; he did it himself: "That's five dollars a carton. We go through a hundred cartons a month. That's five hundred dollars a month, which will save us an extra six thousand a year."

We got his account.

I usually ask about paper because it's the number one office supply people buy. It doesn't make sense to ask about pencils. I'm not going to say, "I can sell you pencils cheaper than wherever you're buying them now," because most people use maybe three pencils a year. And the price is so negligible that no one is going to change vendors to save a penny on a pencil. But paper? That's a big expense.

Law firms use thousands of sheets of paper for every deal they work on. We did a lot of business with many, many law firms. I remember one firm that was working on a closing all night when the lawyers realized they had run out of paper. That's a potential disaster, especially in the middle of the night. They needed more paper, and they needed it immediately, so their administrative staff called us—yes, in the middle of the night—and asked us if we could help.

This administrative assistant begged us to send paper, by any means: Put it in a car, a cab, a limo—whatever needed to be done as long as the received two boxes of paper so they could complete their work in time for the closing the following day.

We did, and we had that customer for life. The law firm never forgot that we came through for them. *That's* great customer service—and that's what businesses today look for. This is especially true for small to medium-sized companies, with a hundred or fewer employees. The giants of industry are more likely to want the lowest prices because they're buying in such great quantity for so many employees, but the smaller companies are looking for a vendor that will jump through hoops for their business. And that's exactly what we did, whenever we could.

We had another client whose CEO was getting ready for a meeting of all his company's national sales reps. A few days before he was supposed to leave, he decided he wanted to give each rep a leather portfolio, with the company name and logo on the cover. He told his administrative assistant, who called us and asked if there was any way we could produce a hundred portfolios in the next few days. We did. That administrative assistant and that CEO never forgot how we were able to pull that rabbit out of a hat, and we had another customer for life.

That kind of rush job happened maybe three or four times a month. One time a client was preparing for a trip to visit his west-coast office, when he decided, again at the eleventh hour, that he needed next-year's calendar. This was some time in the summer, and those calendars don't typically come out until the fall, so none of our vendors even had any yet. But we weren't going to say no to this client because he did a sizeable amount of business with us. The salesman handling his account used his head and checked some retail stores. Mark Cross had what he was looking for. He bought it retail and solved the customer's problem. He was empowered to make the purchase. He went the extra mile, and the company encouraged our people to act that way. Again, we had a customer who never forgot that we came through, and we had a customer for life.

Another customer called me one day and asked if I could provide customer stationery for him. He owned one of *The Thinker* statues by Rodin (who made several versions, in various media and sizes), and this customer wanted to have the image of it in shadow on a thousand sheets of very high-quality paper he had purchased. Obviously, this is not the type of work we do every day, if at all. However, this customer was the CEO of a huge financial firm we did a lot of business with, so we found a way to get it done. In this case, we didn't even charge him for it, and we delivered outstanding customer service. That was how we differentiated ourselves from our competitors.

## HIRE GREAT CUSTOMER-SERVICE PEOPLE TO SUPPORT YOUR SALES STAFF

You may be wondering how we were able to accommodate these last-minute requests. Actually, it was simple—we had terrific customer-service people. When I first started in this business, the salesmen always had a dedicated customer-service person to handle the myriad requests that came up. The reps gave out their personal phone numbers to customers, to show their dedication—which is why they got calls sometimes at all hours of the day and night. This was decades before cell phones and the 24/7 availability that people in business expect today. This type of service wasn't the norm when I had my first company, back in 1972.

When I hired sales reps, I hired them as a team—a rep and his customer-service assistant. The rep handled all the outside sales, the customer-service assistant was his right-hand person who took care of everything else. We paid the customer-service person's salary, and the sales reps also gave them bonuses. This was the way business was conducted back then. When I was hiring sales reps in the 1970s and '80s, many told me they wouldn't come to work for me unless I agreed to also hire their customer-service assistants. That's how we were able to provide phenomenal customer service. It's like the old saying about a happy marriage: "happy wife, happy life." In this case, if the customers were happy because the customer-service reps took care of them, then the sales reps were happy. And when they were, they sold more, which made everybody happy.

This system also usually had a sales figure attached to it: Each sales rep had a dedicated customer-service person for every $1 million he sold. Obviously, the more business he did, the more assistance he needed to ensure his customers received the great service we wanted them to have. If the sales rep sold less than $1 million a year, he usually shared a customer-service person with another salesman. Some salesmen eventually sold so much—$7, $8, $9 million a year—and needed nine support people. That's when we started building teams of sales reps, and the other salesmen who weren't selling as much as the $9 million rep simply benefited from the customer-service support. All were trained to think outside of the box. Take care of the customer first, deal with the expense later.

Over the years, my businesses grew to where a customer-service department worked better than the original two-person teams. As business expanded nationally, we needed to have coverage across the United States, in every time zone, and at all hours of the day and night. Again, this was before cell phones, so once a customer-service person left the office, she wouldn't be able to answer calls, which meant we needed to change the way we did business to accommodate 24-hour service.

One of the most important things we did to ensure great service was to empower our customer-service support people. Years before *empowerment* was a buzzword (or something that any business did), I made sure our salespeople and customer-service teams knew that they should do almost anything to accommodate and satisfy a customer.

That's radically different from the way most businesses are run—whether they are large corporations with a load of bureaucracy or entrepreneurial ventures or even small businesses. Most employees are more comfortable saying no because they're afraid their supervisors, managers, or the company's owner will read them the riot act when they find out what they've done to make a customer happy. I did the opposite: I said yes—always—and I encouraged my people to say yes, too. We would figure out how to cover the cost later. And we always did. If a customer wanted something in an hour, or two hours, we delivered it. Only afterward did we discuss with the salesman how the extra expense was going to be covered.

Most of the time, the customer was happy to pay whatever

additional costs were involved—like the law firm that needed paper in the middle of the night. Those lawyers didn't care how much it cost to get them the paper they needed. They just wanted it delivered. And the firm gladly paid for the cab, or the limo, or the messenger who delivered it; we simply sent them a bill. When you're working on million-dollar lawsuits or contracts, the cost of a messenger service is insignificant. But the fact that we were willing to deliver cartons of paper in the middle of the night was not insignificant at all— those lawyers remembered that we were there for them in their time of need.

Some of you may be thinking, okay, but what about the clients who don't want to pay extra for outstanding customer service? That's a fair question, and even if most customers are willing to pay, it's true that a company could suffer from the other 10 percent. In that case, we worked out some arrangement with the salesperson, after the deal was done. Our salesmen were willing to pay whatever was required to deliver outstanding service to their customers. Keep in mind that many of our men were making half a million to a million dollars a year in commissions. They had no problem covering the cost of keeping their big-ticket customers happy with the occasional extra expense.

Of course, the key word there is *occasional.* Don't get me wrong. We kept track of the special requests, especially if they cost a significant amount of money. We monitored those costs not only for our sake, but for the customers' sake, because some might not have been aware of the extra costs with their special requests.

For example, one of our customer's purchasing agents called us about once a week with something he urgently needed delivered. We always accommodated and delivered what he needed. But as I mentioned earlier, office supplies shouldn't be an urgent-need business.

After six months, we brought these requests to his attention and said something like, "Listen, this has got to stop. You need to get organized because over the past six months, you've cost us $2,000 in special-delivery expenditures." Then we offered to help him plan what he really needed in the future, so that every order wouldn't be a last-minute emergency.

Until things got out of hand, we were willing to go the extra mile—and with no minimum. Too many businesses and too many people say no to special requests, almost instinctively. I think that's a poor way to run a business, so I always say yes to everything—and then I figure out a way to get it done. That's what built my companies' reputations for great customer service. Not every business can compete on price—especially not commodities businesses—so you have to find another way to excel. Passion and dedication to outstanding service are terrific differentiators.

## REMEMBER: YOUR CUSTOMER IS ALWAYS RIGHT

I also believe the customer is always right. That used to be a cliché, but I think many people and companies no longer subscribe to this idea. They think it's old-fashioned. For example, in his best-selling book, *The 4-Hour Workweek*, Tim Ferriss wrote how draining it was for him to try to accommodate all of his customers' requests and demands. He says his life and business improved dramatically when he told customers that they needed to either do business his way or take it elsewhere. Although I agree that you shouldn't allow your customers to mistreat you, I still believe the customer is always right, and I try to accommodate my customers whenever possible.

I also allow customers to return products at any time. For

example, I had a customer who ordered blue binders for her office. When they arrived, she called her sales rep and told him she didn't like the shade of blue because it was different from what she saw in our catalog. The salesman looked at her account and saw that her company bought a quarter-of-a-million dollars' worth of products from us every year, so of course we were willing to take back a four-dollar binder, even if she ordered hundreds of them!

Moreover, many times, we didn't even ask the customer to return the products. We created a policy: If the return was less than twenty dollars, the customer could keep the product, at no charge, because it cost more to pick it up and return it. We know returns are a hassle for many customers, and if it's a custom product, we can't resell it anyway—for example, in the case of these binders, they had the name of the customer's company on the cover. We told the buyer to give them away to other departments or employees in her company. Keep in mind that it also costs my company time to receive the returned goods, unpack them, inventory them, and put them back on the shelves—all in the hopes that some future employee of this company will want the shade of blue that this buyer didn't like. That's a long shot, so better for her to simply keep them, and we'll provide the shade of blue she really wants.

Obviously, there were factors we considered when deciding how to handle this situation. One was the high volume of products this customer bought from us every year. However, even with low-volume customers, we were happy to accept returns, with no minimum dollar attached. A more important factor was whether a customer was taking advantage of us. We monitored our returns, and when we found customers who had very high percentages of returned goods, we brought that to their attention.

For example, we had one customer who returned 62 percent of everything his company bought. That's a lot of returns, and it was costing us a fortune. I requested a meeting with the purchasing agent, and I showed her the pattern of returns. When she saw how much her company was sending back, she was shocked. I explained to her that we simply couldn't afford that. We needed to figure out a way to order the correct items in the first place. She understood.

We also understood how these mistakes happen. Sometimes it was because the customer's employees had flipped through our catalog and ordered whatever they wanted. When their boss saw something on their desks that wasn't essential and asked about it, the employee didn't want to admit to the boss that he or she had ordered it intentionally. Instead, the employee might tell the boss it was ordered or delivered by mistake, in which case the boss said, "Return it."

Other times, something actually was ordered by mistake. Someone orders something, thinking there are ten in a box, but there are actually a hundred. She ordered ten boxes, but she didn't need a thousand; she only needed a hundred. That meant she wanted to return nine boxes. We know that's going to happen, and we accommodate returns whenever we can. Returns are part of the business. Typically, returns affected us by about a point and a half a year, so if we were selling $10 million a year, returns were a $150,000 mistake. But we had to regulate it because if 1.5 percent became 5 percent, then we might have gone out of business. We monitored and worked with our customers so that returns didn't get out of hand for either of us. That monitoring benefited both of us.

We then went to their wholesaler, from whom we purchased $100 million of product per year, and we negotiated a percentage allowance for the returns that we took back from customers. It cost the wholesaler the same amount that it cost us to pick it up, handle the return, and issue credits. This completed the cycle and reduced our exposures to the cost of returns.

Delivering outstanding customer service created terrific, long-term relationships with our customers. We catered to them, and they were loyal to us. That loyalty is priceless. We built on our customers' loyalty by developing loyalty with our employees, as I'll describe in the next chapter.

## *BUILD RELATIONSHIPS WITH YOUR CUSTOMERS:*

1. *Be passionate about your business: That enthusiasm appeals to customers.* People will naturally be drawn to you if you're upbeat about how you can help them do their work more efficiently or productively.

2. *Sell constantly to everyone you meet, and continuously expand your network.* Look for customers in every organization you belong to (religious, social, philanthropic, business), ask who *they* know, and develop reciprocal relationships with people you do business with.

3. *Ask people if they're happy with their current vendors.* Listen for clues that someone may be looking for a better price, better service, or a more reliable vendor—then offer to help them because their business will also help yours.

4. *Go the extra mile for customers, and say yes whenever you can.* Go out of your way to accommodate customers. They'll remember that forever, and you'll have customers for life.

5. *Hire great salespeople and customer service people, and empower them to say yes, too.* Find the best salespeople or find people with potential and train them to be the best; then make sure they have the support they need to deliver great service.

# THREE

# DEVELOP LOYALTY WITH YOUR EMPLOYEES

*I* DEVELOPED MY BASIC PHILOSOPHY OF HOW TO work with people and treat employees by learning what not to do. I had a bad experience while I was working at one of my father's companies during a summer break from college. My father had a young man named Marvin working for him—someone who was older than I was, but younger than my father—and my father gave Marvin the opportunity to be the president of the company. It was understood that after I graduated from college, I would join that firm in a partnership role. I wasn't going to take over Marvin's job, but I would have some leadership role.

Marvin and I worked well together during the summers while I was in college. After I graduated, Nancy and I got married, and Marvin attended our wedding. But when I got back from my honeymoon and showed up for work at this company, Marvin said to me, "Who said you could work here?" I was confused, so that night, I asked my father, "Am I missing something?" I think what happened is that someone must have said to Marvin, "Someday, Howard's father is going to replace you and put his son in charge." But that was *never* my father's intention.

My father met with Marvin and clarified the situation, telling him, "Your job is secure. You will always be the president of this company unless you do something stupid. If you don't do something stupid, you will be the boss. My son is going to be a partner only from a shareholder point of view. He's not going to tell you what to do. If you want to develop a relationship and work with him, that will benefit you and the company. If not, then you're going to create a problem, and if my son says he's leaving the company, then you and I are going to have a problem." Sometimes, the problem disappears if you explain it well.

After that conversation, Marvin and I worked peacefully together for five years. In 1970, my father sold all of his companies. The new owners wanted us to stay for a while in order to make sure the hand-off in leadership and management went smoothly. Marvin stayed on for another year, and I stayed on for almost two. I don't really know what Marvin did after he left that company; I never heard from him again. We had worked together, but we were never really friends.

## DON'T BE BOSSY (EVEN WHEN YOU'RE THE BOSS)

I started looking for a business to buy, and that's when I bought into my first company, Summit Office Supply. From my very first day at Summit, and because of the negative experience I had had with Marvin, I tried to sell myself to Summit's employees, to show them I wasn't coming in as their boss, but as a fellow worker learning a business I knew nothing about. It became natural for me to try and show people who I was, what my goals were, and how I needed their help to learn the business and how they did their work.

I did the same thing for the rest of my career. Whenever I bought a company, I spoke to the owners and tried to convince them to stay on as salespeople. I showed them that they could make more money selling for me than they had made by owning the company, and I told them I had no problem with them making more money than me because their success would help the bottom line of the company. There wasn't any jealousy involved.

Because I had started in an adversarial role with Marvin at my first job, I learned a valuable lesson about management and leadership. I decided that when I was in a position to work with people, I was going to go out of my way to demonstrate how important they were to me. By doing that, I hoped they would reciprocate. I didn't state that idea aloud, but I believe my first poor experience in management at my father's company led me to develop my ideas about how I wanted to manage people. I wanted to treat people the opposite of how I had been treated. And that approach paid off not only for me but for so many people I worked with over the years.

## SHOW YOUR WORK ETHIC

In general, I led by example. Soon after I bought into Summit, I realized I wasn't happy with how the staff processed orders. They weren't working as productively or as fast as I thought they should. One of the other executives and I worked on the floor on Wednesday nights, and we took orders alongside the rest of the staff. We worked hard and I made sure we picked faster than everybody else;

my goal was to motivate the regular warehouse staff, to work faster to show us they were better than us.

It worked. We picked up the productivity. As the business grew and orders increased, we had to get more out of the workers. When we had only twenty orders a day, it wasn't as important for them to work quickly and efficiently. However, once we started getting hundreds and eventually thousands of orders a day, everyone needed to work as productively as possible.

I also managed by being visible on all floors, came in at 4:00 a.m. and let them know I was paying attention to how people were doing, walking around, long before that was a buzzword. Every day, I walked the floor of all my companies. I wanted to get to know the people I worked with, and I wanted them to get to know me. I've always believed that the best way to do that is to see and be seen, and at least to say hello to everyone I passed. We only had ten employees when I bought Summit. Over the years, that number grew to twenty, then to fifty, and finally to a hundred and fifty employees when I sold the business to BT.

I walked through the warehouse every day at different times; I wanted to make sure that people knew I cared about how the place looked. I'm a perfectionist about cleanliness and order. That might be a result of my years at Valley Forge Military Academy, or this trait might be something innate. When everything in an office and a warehouse is put away in an orderly, well-organized way, I think that makes a statement about who you are, as the company owner or manager, and how you run your business. I believe it shows that you run an efficient business. I wanted people who saw our offices and warehouses to be impressed so they wouldn't forget it.

## THANK EMPLOYEES AND DON'T CRITICIZE IN PUBLIC

I also made it a point to thank anyone who had done an outstanding job. Every night when I left the office, I brought home the billing and the open orders. I didn't have time to look at these during the day, so I reviewed them at night. I've always been good with numbers, and if I saw an order that was unusually large, I would remember it, line for line, and I thanked the warehouse people for getting it out so fast. I thanked the salesman who had brought it in.

When I first started doing this, the salesmen were always surprised when I thanked them for bringing in a large order. I felt it was important to give credit where credit was due. I've talked to too many people who say they never received recognition for their work, and that wasn't the way I wanted to run my business.

I tried not to criticize employees publicly. Nobody is perfect, and when people make mistakes, I think it's important to teach them why they made the mistake and let them know you hope they learn from them. In fact, I believe people make mistakes and can truly learn from that experience. If they keep making the same mistake, that's a different story.

However, some of my salesmen didn't always listen to me because they thought they knew more than I did. At times, this backfired and they lost an account. They begged me to help by taking the owner or manager out for dinner and of course, I did. It was in our best interest to keep clients happy. But, I also let the salesperson know he had made a mistake.

I didn't yell at anyone it in the middle of the office; I talked to them in my office, with the door closed. I didn't yell at people often, but I'm not a saint. Still, in general, I tried to treat people well. My father often told me, "It's all in the explanation." In other words, if I explained something but the person didn't understand, that's not that person's fault; it's mine. I didn't explain it properly or adequately. I went out of my way to explain things well the first time and the second time. If I had to explain something a third time, though I tried, I might not have been as gentle and considerate as before.

## PAY ATTENTION TO WHAT'S IMPORTANT

I believe the most important people in a company are your customer service people and your truck drivers. These front-line people are the first people—and sometimes, the only people—with whom your customers interact face to face. As the old saying goes, you only get one chance to make a first impression, so your customer-facing employees especially should be professional, polite, courteous, and helpful.

Keep in mind that when someone gets a delivery from UPS, for example, that driver or delivery person works for UPS. However, when my customers received deliveries from us, those deliveries were made by our people driving my trucks.

I learned how important our drivers are from my customers. If a truck driver dressed sloppily or looked dirty or had an attitude or, God forbid, was drunk, I heard about it immediately. Perhaps the driver delivered an order and the customer asked him to move something, or take a carton of paper to another floor, and the driver said, "That's not my job." When something like that happened, the customer called me and said, "You'd better fire that driver, or I'll find someone else to buy from." I was in a commodity business, and my customers could buy pens and paper anywhere—in bookstores, drug stores, supermarkets, and many other places—so my company needed to excel in customer service.

A driver with a bad attitude is a real problem. A driver might have an argument with his or her spouse before coming to work, which would put them in a bad mood all day. That bad attitude might cost me twenty customers that day. That's not something we could condone. I need my people to be professional, even when they're having personal problems. The first time I got a complaint about someone, I gave that person a warning. But if there was another complaint in a short amount of time, I had to let them go.

I sat down with many drivers over the years and explained to them how important they were, that they were the people who most often came in one-to-one contact with our customers. Our customer-service people did business over the phone, so there's no eye contact or face-to-face interaction at all with customers. Our truck drivers and delivery people were often the face of the company, and it was critical they be polite, friendly, and considerate of our customers. If our driver greets our customers with a smile and says, "Have a nice weekend" or asks, "What else can I do for you?" or, "Is there anything you need when I go back to the office?" it goes a long way. Since there's nothing that differentiated my company in terms of our products, we needed to go the extra mile in service. When you're selling a commodity, everyone who comes in contact with your customers has to make a great impression.

When I bought a company, the salespeople typically told me that the most important people they relied on were the truck drivers. The drivers know the routes, and they know what time each customer expects his or her deliveries. With some customers, it doesn't matter what time they receive their orders, so the driver can deliver at two or three in the afternoon. But there are also customers who want their orders delivered first thing in the morning.

As a result, if that truck driver left our company, or if we started routing the trucks differently because we didn't know what the driver knew, we would start having problems. Therefore, I felt it was critical to always make sure our drivers were happy and knew there were better opportunities in the company they were joining. When I acquired a company, I wanted all the customer service and salespeople to feel the same.

## OFFER TO HELP

In every business I was in, I knew everyone's name and I became friendly with the employees. If someone needed help, I helped. It's usually pretty obvious when someone is worried or stressed, and whenever I noticed that, I asked if there was something I could do to help them. Sometimes it was a financial problem; sometimes it was a health problem—the employee's own health or someone in their family. I was fortunate to have money, so if someone was in a pinch or needed an advance on his or her paycheck, I offered to help.

Managers and especially business owners are usually in a stronger position financially than their employees. This may seem obvious, but it never fails to surprise me how few business owners are willing to help their employees when they most need it.

We had employees who had families in other countries, and when someone died, especially a parent, they obviously wanted to attend the funeral. That type of travel is usually not planned for, and it's often very expensive. There were many times when an employee asked me for time off to attend a funeral, and they knew they could ask to borrow money from me for the plane fare. I always lent it, and there was nothing formal about these loans—nothing they had to sign. We simply made a gentleman's agreement, and they always paid me back because they appreciated that I had helped them in their time of need.

I also helped when my employees were having health problems. I knew many doctors because of my daughter Michele's health issues, and my employees knew they could ask me to recommend someone who could help. I was happy to do this, and I know my help saved at least one person's life. Very serious medical problems often require immediate help from the best doctors, at the best hospitals, and I was fortunate to know many capable and highly-qualified physicians and surgeons, so I shared my personal network with my employees who needed it.

When you treat people well, they're more likely going to be loyal to you. I've found that to be true throughout my career. I had people work with me for twenty, twenty-five, even thirty years at various companies. Even when I sold a company that had a restrictive covenant which prevented me from working in the industry, when I came back to the industry, many of them joined me in my next business. Even when they went to work for other companies out of necessity while I was waiting for my restrictive covenant to expire, many of them left those jobs and came back to me. Even when business got tough and we couldn't pay our bills, they stayed loyal.

And, to this day, they're still loyal. Even though I'm retired, I still keep up with so many people, and if I can help them or advise them in any way, I'm happy to do so. Loyalty is a two-way street, and I'm very grateful and appreciative for all my friends and associates. I can't emphasize enough how important loyalty is. I truly believe that business success comes from loyalty to your customers, loyalty to your vendors, and loyalty to your employees. With that trifecta, you almost can't fail!

## DEVELOP LOYALTY WITH YOUR EMPLOYEES:

1. ***Don't be arrogant; be open to learning from your employees.*** They'll appreciate your attitude, and they'll be more likely to work well with you and become loyal employees.

2. ***Let your employees know how important they are.*** If your employees make a poor impression on your customers, you may lose that business forever, so don't let that happen.

3. ***Get to know your people.*** The better you know your employees, the better your relationships will be, and you'll create an environment where people want to do great work.

4. ***Help your employees when they have problems—financially or otherwise.*** Lending money or providing access to professionals you know generates good will and loyalty.

# FOUR

# BE LOYAL TO YOUR VENDORS

*M*OST PEOPLE CAN SEE THE BENEFIT OF LOYALTY to customers. After all, repeat business is much easier to maintain than finding new customers, so everyone wants to keep customers they've already won. Similarly, most people agree that having strong, long-term relationships with loyal employees is beneficial for everyone since your employees know how your company operates, and they know your customers. However, some people don't see the benefit in being loyal to their vendors. They may even believe that it's beneficial to *not* be loyal, so they can shop around for the better deal. I disagree.

## TAKE THE LONG VIEW

I believe the best deals came from long-term relationships with my vendors, so that I could draw on those relationships in good times and bad. I took the long view, which benefited my companies and my vendors. I believe we all made more money.

Some people may not see the benefit of doing business with you when you're just starting out. I was very open about my interest in developing long-term relationships with my vendors. From my earliest days in business, I told them I expected to stay with them as my company grew. The more competitive they made us, the more business we would get and, therefore, the more business they would get. In fact, I used to kid them by saying, "This train is leaving the station. If you're willing to take a ride on it and you're good to us— if you keep us competitive, we're going to stick with you. But we'd better not find out, either by accident or when we buy another company, that you're not giving us the best price. There's no reason for us to be loyal to you if you're not going to treat us properly."

In short, there were no free lunches. For example, if we were buying binders at, say, a dollar a binder, and we found out that the vendor was selling to another office-supply company for only ninety-five cents, not only did we raise hell but we expected them to reimburse us the difference for at least a year. If they didn't agree to that, we would stop buying from them and find another vendor. Loyalty works both ways. Our vendors couldn't expect that my company would continue to buy from them if they didn't sell to us at competitive prices. We were loyal to our vendors, and we expected them to treat us honorably in return.

That scenario actually happened after I sold my first company, Summit, to BT, the Dutch company that wanted to expand into the U.S. market. The Dutch managers asked me to stay on and continue to manage BT Summit. Over the fifteen years that I had owned it, I had increased the company's annual revenues from $300,000 to $55 million. After Summit became part of BT, we grew to a $400 million company, and we were still buying from the same companies. Why? Because I was loyal to my vendors.

We had also acquired some smaller companies, including a little company in Texas that was doing $30 million a year. In the course of our due diligence on that acquisition, we discovered that the Texas company was getting a better price than we were from our binder vendor on indexes, which are the tabbed separators that are typically used with binders. So, I called the vendor and told him what we had found: "During our due diligence, we saw that we're paying eighty-five cents and the Texas company is paying sixty-eight cents. That's a savings of seventeen cents for each set of indexes. Based on last year's volume of what we bought from you, I think you owe us $250,000."

The vendor replied, "Well, that must be a mistake." So I showed him the bills, and numbers don't lie. I asked him if he wanted me to call his competitor in the index business and offer him not only the business that Summit had been doing with the first vendor, but also the Texas company's business (since we had acquired it), and the Dutch company's business (since it had acquired Summit).

At this, the vendor said, "No, no, no. We'll reimburse you the $250,000." And he did.

Again, I made it clear from the outset that I would be loyal to my vendors, but I also would not tolerate it if they weren't being fair to my company, in terms of pricing. Business relationships are like a marriage: You can't cheat on your husband or wife and expect that there won't be any consequences. In a good marriage, you will be loyal to your spouse, in good times and in bad.

## STICK WITH VENDORS WHO STAND BY YOU

I honored that loyalty by refusing to change vendors who were loyal
to me. Every year, their competitors came to me saying they could
offer me a better deal than the vendor I was currently buying from. I
always listened to the proposal, then I went back to my current vendor to give them the last right of refusal. Market conditions change,
and sometimes a loyal vendor who is treating your company properly may not be competitive based on these conditions.

My vendor's competitors wanted to do business with my company because, as they told me, "You're a different company now.
You're so much bigger, and you're financially stronger." When I
heard this, I thought, *Where were you when I needed you three years
ago?* I told them I had given them the same opportunity I gave the
vendors I was buying from. "This company took that ride on the
train when it was leaving the station. It's on the track; it's loyal to
me; it's performing, so I have no reason to change vendors. If you
can offer me something special or unusual, let me know. But I'm
not going to change vendors just because you want my business now
that I'm bigger."

My vendors appreciated that, and they were willing to work
with me when I was smaller and doing less business. They believed
that I would grow, and they agreed that as I did more business,
they would do more business, too. What started as a $300,000
company, grew to a $55 million company, and by the time I'd left
in 1996, we'd grown to $1.5 billion. That's a lot of business for a
vendor to lose. It was incumbent on them to go overboard to make
sure we remained competitive, because, again, they would receive
the business of every new account we won, and they would lose the
business of every account we lost. This is especially important if

you're growing your business. If you're not growing your business, then it is what it is and nothing more.

After I sold my first two businesses, I faced the same challenge. I called my vendors and explained that I was starting something new, and I asked them to once again get on the train with me. I said, "I'm back. I don't have the volume yet, but I wonder how you're going to treat me. Before, I was doing $400 million in annual sales, and now I'm only a $2 million business. But I plan to grow this company just like I grew the last one. So again—are you prepared to risk not being on the train that's leaving the station?" That was in March 2010. By November 2010, I had bought My Office Products (MYOP), which was doing $120 million.

Over the years, I learned that even when I was getting a great price from my vendors, they almost always were able to go even lower than what they were charging me. I discovered this when Summit was acquired by BT, which had also acquired other stationery businesses in the United States. As I mentioned before, BT asked me to stay on, which I did, and I not only ran the company but was in charge of purchasing, with a full staff. That gave me a bird's-eye view of how the vendors I had been doing business with had been selling to my competitors because BT now owned some of those former competitors.

That showed me that the vendors really had no bottom, and as a company grew larger and the competition became stiffer, the vendors were more willing to bend over backwards. Of course, I knew that they were selling at lower prices to Office Depot and Staples, which were doing several billions of dollars a year and adding retail stores like crazy. I knew I couldn't get the same prices the giants were getting, but I needed to know that I was at least competitive.

My relationships with my vendors lasted as long as I was in control of my companies. After I sold a business, many of my vendors thought that they could continue to sell to it. Unfortunately, that didn't happen. I sold my last company, HiTouch, to Staples. If my suppliers were not already selling to Staples, those vendors had no chance of becoming Staples' suppliers because Staples negotiated prices the same way I did. Staples' philosophy was to say, "If we find out that you were selling to a smaller company at a lower price, you'll never do business with us again." That was a bigger threat to vendors than anything I ever asked for, just because of Staples' enormous size. Staples was obviously in the driver's seat because it was the largest company in the industry, with $26 billion in annual sales. The next-largest company was Office Depot, which did $10 billion, and then there were companies like mine that did $300 million or $400 million. That's a big difference. But most of their products were privately branded and purchased overseas.

When I sold my third company to Staples, I thought Staples had a 5 to 6 percent overall advantage, pricewise, over us. But I found out very quickly that Staples actually had at least a 10 to 15 percent advantage over us. That was really an eye opener, which only proved that we never had the best price. Nevertheless, we wanted to make sure we were as competitive as we could be. And as much as they could, my vendors complied because they were afraid that if we caught them selling at lower prices to other companies, then we would change vendors. They realized they had to create a domestic brand without the frills—for instance, a plain white box—to compete with overseas products. They worked with us because, as always, if we lost the business, they lost the business. We were in business together.

If my vendors wanted to continue to stay with me after I sold my business, they knew that we were going to get a better price, so they had to sharpen their pencils. For example, if they were selling me a binder for a dollar each, and another company came in at ninety-four cents each, then my vendor came back and offered ninety-five cents, I wasn't going to cut them out for a penny a piece. I respected the loyalty that those vendors had earned over the years that we'd been in business together. And although a penny might not seem like a lot of money, when you buy five million binders a year, that's a lot of pennies adding up.

I realize other companies might say, "I can't afford to be loyal. Business is too cut-throat today, so if another vendor comes to me and offers to sell to me for less than I'm currently paying, I'm going to change vendors." If that's how that company wants to do business, that's fine, but that wasn't the way I did it. I knew I always had pricing I didn't deserve, so I felt I had to be loyal to the vendors who gave me that pricing, who would in turn be loyal to me.

## ASK FOR HELP WHEN YOU NEED IT MOST

My loyalty to vendors paid off enormously whenever times were tough or unstable. The worst of these occurred in 2001. In March of that year, my second company, Allied, moved into a new 275,000-square-foot warehouse, located in Clifton, New Jersey. It had state-of-the-art conveyors and technology, similar to what FedEx uses today. In April, we moved our corporate offices into a 60,000-square-foot building next door to the warehouse. We chose this location because of its proximity to New York City, where we had an enormous base of customers—and potential customers. In our business, when we went to get a new account, the buyers always wanted to see our office and our warehouse, meet our staff, and know what our added-value proposition was.

Clifton is very close to all of the routes connecting North Jersey and New York City: the Lincoln Tunnel, the Holland Tunnel, and the George Washington Bridge. If a NYC-based company had an emergency and needed a product, we could ship it from our Clifton warehouse to the NYC location, on our own trucks, in an hour, maybe a little more. In contrast, our biggest competitor was a company also in New Jersey, but much farther west, near Hackettstown, which would be lucky to get something into NYC in an hour and a half; more likely, it would take two to two and a half hours. When potential customers visited our competitor and had to fight the traffic back into the city, they worried about how much time that company would need to deliver their merchandise. That didn't happen when they left our warehouse.

However, when we moved into the new corporate offices and the new warehouse, we soon found we were over-extended. Obviously, the new warehouse wasn't full on day one; we contracted for that much space so that we could grow our business, or acquire more companies, over the next five to ten years. We were planning for the future.

Unfortunately, on September 11, 2001, that future literally came crashing down when the terrorists attacked New York City and Washington, D.C. We had many customers in the two World Trade Towers—mostly law firms and advertising agencies. Cantor Fitzgerald, a financial firm specializing in the bond market, was one of our biggest accounts, and as everyone who lived through September 11th remembers, Cantor Fitzgerald suffered the greatest loss of life when its entire office was destroyed by the plane that hit the 93rd to 99ᵗʰ floors. Of the 2,996 deaths that day, 2,606 happened in the Trade Towers, and 658 of those were people who worked for Cantor Fitzgerald. None of Cantor Fitzgerald's staff working that day in the Towers survived.

The loss of life was staggering, and the outpouring of grief was overwhelming, as people searched and prayed that their loved ones had been spared. In the days that followed, many businesses came to a virtual standstill as America reeled from its first attack since Pearl Harbor. That standstill was appropriate given the enormity of the tragedy. Eventually, though, we needed to get back to work, to go on living. For many of us in the New York area, we needed the distraction of work to create some sense of normalcy in our lives again.

However, we soon realized there was a new normal because when the World Trade Center collapsed, so did many of the businesses that had been located in the Twin Towers and the immediate surrounding areas. I was grateful I hadn't lost any family or friends on that terrible day, and my heart went out to all those who did. Still, I lost business—$11 million worth of business that would never come back because those customers' companies were wiped out.

Moreover, it was almost impossible to go back to business as usual, which didn't even exist anymore because of the devastation in lower Manhattan. The rubble from two 110-story towers of concrete, steel, and glass was enormous, and city officials set up barricades to keep people out while they searched for survivors and tried to make the area safe again. As a result, we couldn't make deliveries south of 14ᵗʰ Street for at least the next six months, which wiped out another $20 million or so of our lost business.

I realize our $30 million loss pales in comparison to the loss of almost 3,000 lives and the effect that loss had on their families and friends and colleagues, but as the owner of a company, I had 700 people depending on me for their continued livelihood. I needed to take care of them, and I didn't know how I was going to do that. We were a $300 million business at the time, and if this 10 percent loss had been the result of a more ordinary business event, we would have been able to recover more easily. But there was no insurance for this. We had lost customers and the receivables that were not collectible because the people weren't there—literally, and tragically—and it wasn't possible to bring them back.

The optimism that had led us to move six months earlier into a huge new warehouse and corporate offices had turned to apprehension. We couldn't pay our bills. We also couldn't get credit to buy the new merchandise we needed for our customers.

This was when the loyalty we had shown to our vendors for so many years proved invaluable. I had been in the business for thirty years by the time of the September 11th attacks, so I had strong, long-term relationships I knew I could depend on.

I started calling our vendors to see if they could help us. As the president of my company, I didn't call the credit managers; I knew they would have to follow their companies' policies and wouldn't be authorized to bend them. Instead, I called the CEOs, presidents, or owners and appealed to them directly. Then we had an industry meeting where several of our vendors—ACCO, S.P. Richards, and 3M—were part of a committee on credit. They stood up for us by telling all the other suppliers, "We are giving Brown ninety days' credit because he has given us his word that he'll be able to pay the bill on the ninetieth day. We hope that all of you will extend a minimum of sixty days and try to extend to ninety days, if you can. We hope you'll stand behind him until his company can get back on its feet."

If my suppliers hadn't given us that time—if, instead, they had squeezed me, they could have put me out of business. They also would have lost all of their receivables. When I gave my word we would pay them by the ninetieth day, we had that extra time to recover.

There were those who turned their backs on us. We ended our relationships with them and switched to their competitors. When we got back on our feet, many of those vendors approached me and tried to do business with me again, saying, "We were there for you in the beginning." I told them, "But you almost put me out of business because you turned your back on us." There was nothing they could do that would persuade me to do business with them again. Loyalty is not a short-term factor; it needs to be demonstrated over many years.

## GET TO KNOW THE RIGHT PEOPLE

Loyalty is a balancing act. Also, you need to bear in mind who you're being loyal to because the person you've been loyal to may not always be in charge. When somebody new comes in, that person may not know you from Adam. For every company you do business with, you need to consider who you're going to be working with, who the dealmaker and decision maker is.

That's one reason I always wanted to deal with the top, either the company owner or the C-suite. Another reason is that I wanted to make deals with someone who would be at the company for the long term. Whenever I thought I was dealing with someone who was going to be with the company for a short time, I tried to include and communicate with the next two people reporting to that person. I wanted to ensure that they were part of every discussion we had.

It's important to evaluate the person you're dealing with because when you demonstrate that level of loyalty and commitment, you want the person and the company you're doing business with to understand, respect, and honor that loyalty. I wanted to be sure I was dealing with somebody who was reputable and a long-term player, someone I had a future with.

With some vendors I bought from, however, there was a revolving door of people. One company had five different CEOs in seven years. It's difficult to develop a long-term relationship with a company if the CEO or president is changing constantly. In situations like that, the only way to protect your business is to make sure you have iron-clad contracts in place, which we did, so the new CEO can't change the deal you made with the previous CEO.

I continue to advise people in business about the benefits of developing long-term, loyal relationships with their vendors. For example, one entrepreneur I know well sells building materials and supplies. One of his wholesalers is owned by Home Depot, who is also his competitor on about 50 percent of his products. He wasn't getting the terms he wanted because of this situation, and when he explained to me what was happening, I realized he was dealing with a salesperson who didn't have the authority to offer him a better deal.

I suggested he ask the salesman to arrange a meeting with the president of the company. He needed to meet with the president and make him aware of the fact that the previous year, he had bought $9 million from this company; this year, he was buying $12 million; and next year, he expected to buy $15 million.

My friend needed to do what I described at the beginning of this chapter. He needed to tell his vendors that the more *his* company grows, the more *their* businesses will grow, so they should try to give him a better deal.

Sure enough, he got on a plane and went to that wholesaler's headquarters, met with the president, and got his better deal. That will be the beginning of a beautiful, long-term, and loyal relationship.

In short, you have to know who you're dealing with, and whenever possible, you should try to deal with the highest-level person you can. Once somebody gives you their word and keeps it, a pattern of trust emerges. Loyalty is critical to your customers, to your employees, and to the companies you buy from. If you don't have all three, you're in a lot of trouble, no matter what business you're in.

## BE LOYAL TO YOUR VENDORS:

1. **Take the long view.** Every business has downturns and losses, but if you've been loyal to the companies you buy from, they're more likely to be there when you need a helping hand.

2. **Show your vendors how they benefit from a long-term relationship.** Emphasize that as you do better and increase your business, so will they because you'll be buying more from them.

3. **Let your vendors know there's no free lunch.** If a vendor has offered a better deal to one of your competitors, that vendor needs to make up for that, to continue to do business with you.

4. **Ask for help when you need it.** When your business is in trouble, ask your vendors to cut you some slack. If you've been loyal, they should be willing to help until you recover.

5. **Establish relationships with the most senior person you can get to.** It's easier to develop loyalty with the C-suite or owner because that person has ultimate decision-making authority.

# FIVE

# DIFFERENTIATE YOUR PRODUCTS BY ADDING VALUE AND OFFERING GREAT SERVICE

*W*HEN I FIRST WENT INTO BUSINESS, SUMMIT Office Supply was a small company. We did only $300,000 in annual sales when I bought it in 1972. There were no big-box office supply stores back then. Staples and Office Depot didn't come on the scene until 1986, and OfficeMax was founded in 1988. However, there still were other companies that sold office supplies much larger than Summit, like New Jersey Office Supply. Because we were small, and in a commodity business, we needed to find a way to differentiate ourselves from them.

## OFFER YOUR CUSTOMERS ONE-STOP SHOPPING FOR EVERYTHING THEY NEED

I realized the best way we could do that was to provide superior service to our customers. We tried to convince them to buy anything they needed from us. We wanted to be a one-stop shop. Even if we didn't carry something, we got it for them. For example, we didn't carry typewriters (which were still being used in offices during the 1980s), but if one of our customers wanted a typewriter, we found and delivered it.

We started by offering printing because, back then, there was a print shop on almost every street corner in Manhattan. Since Summit was also located in Manhattan, we could get printing done immediately, from many different print shops. Printing was also a natural line extension of office supplies. When a few of our customers said yes to our printing suggestion, we kept expanding our offerings. We saw that this approach was getting us more and more business, and we started pushing what we called the "one-solution sell."

We also offered to warehouse customers' custom-office products, another way we differentiated ourselves from other suppliers. By warehousing their merchandise, we made those supplies available to customers within hours, which many of our customers appreciated. If they had an office that forgot to order sales slips, or promotional items, they could get them from us immediately.

We offered warehousing in two ways: bill-and-hold or bill-and-ship. With bill-and-hold, customers paid right away for all the merchandise they ordered, and we shipped in whatever increments they wanted us to ship, for whenever they needed it. With the bill-and-ship program, customers ordered in large quantities, we warehoused all of it, and they paid us only for the amounts that we shipped to them when they wanted it.

Letterhead was a big print item for many law firms. They wanted to order in bulk because that reduced their printing cost, but they didn't want to warehouse huge amounts of letterhead because it took up so much space. The bill-and-hold arrangement proved a great deal for them. They'd pay us up front for say, a 100,000 copies of their custom letterhead and matching envelopes, and we would warehouse it for them. When they needed letterhead, they simply sent us a memo for how much they wanted, even if it was for much smaller quantities. We delivered as little as one box of five hundred sheets right away, already paid for. They didn't need to worry that they had run out, or it had gotten damaged, or waterlogged, which often happened when customers kept supplies in their own basements. We stored their documents in our state-of the art warehouses.

Some customers were concerned that something might happen to our warehouses that would affect the items we were storing for them. To prevent that, we kept a backup supply of their inventory in different warehouses around the country. We didn't want them to worry about fire or a power failure or any other catastrophic event that could prevent them from getting what they needed. We had one warehouse in Long Island and another in Boston, among others, so we could always deliver their items the same day they ordered them. Our customers loved that we had a backup plan, and we were fortunate that in all the years we were in business, we never once needed to implement it.

Many of our customers were banks, which used to give away a coffeepot or some other token item to anyone opening a new account. We warehoused those items, as well as pens and lollipops like those the banks gave out to their customers' children. As long as we received a purchase order to cover those items, we would warehouse them for our customers until they needed something.

When we delivered those items, the customer received only a single carton with everything inside—one delivery, one bill. That saved customers money when they processed their bills because they didn't have to create purchase orders for three or four different vendors, which was somewhat disruptive. Instead, we had one driver delivering one box with everything they ordered.

Many banks had between eight and thirty branches, and they needed supplies for all those locations. We convinced them to allow us to print their proprietary printed materials and promotional products in advance, and we treated those as commodity items. They'd give us a purchase order for these, and if they didn't use what we had printed for them, they'd have to buy it from us at our cost plus the profit we would have made, not at the cost alone. The benefit for the banks was that we delivered to them only what they needed when they needed it, and we billed them only when we delivered it. The inventory expense was on our books, not their books, which again created added value for our customers.

## DON'T GET COMPLACENT: ALWAYS TRY TO SELL MORE

I tried to make inroads into new products whenever I could. One of my bank customers had thirty-five branches. I was one of the original shareholders in the bank, and over the years, I became very friendly with the CEO. During that time, we sold the bank coffee and beverages, which the branches offered to their customers, and all the printing that was specific to each branch—their business cards, letterhead, envelopes, etc., all of which we warehoused for them.

Then I asked the CEO if I could provide the bank's promotional products—the pens and other items that the bank gave to people when they opened new accounts. He told me he had another client who handled the bank's promotional items, which amounted to about $1.5 million of products. I asked if that company warehoused those items for the bank, and the CEO said, "No. We keep them in our basements. And there have been times when we have run out of something at one of our branches, so we have to run out and make a last-minute delivery."

I made him an offer: "If you give me 40 percent of that business, I'll take in all of the other company's products—the other 60 percent—into my warehouse. The vendor can bill me what you pay her, and I won't charge you anything for warehousing it. But the next time you reorder, I'd like the opportunity to sell those products to you, and I'll charge you less money than you're paying now." I knew I could do this because he showed me his bills; I saw what he was paying for those products, and I saw what she was charging him for freight to deliver them. When I asked him if he would consider giving me some of that business, he said, "Of course."

Over time, we got 100 percent of his business because we created added value for the bank, saved him money, and provided better controls. He didn't have to warehouse those products anymore, and he paid for them only when they were delivered to each bank branch location. But as he expanded to more branches or more banks, it was an easy transition because we were already part of the solution and had inventory to cover his new branches or acquisitions.

## BE INNOVATIVE: ANTICIPATE WHAT YOUR CUSTOMERS NEED

Another value-added service we provided was shredding. After I sold Allied, I had a restrictive covenant that prevented me from working in the office-supply industry for four years. Although I was sixty-one years old and was in a financial position to retire, I wasn't ready to yet. Instead, I bought a company called Rentacrate, which, as the name tells you, rented crates to companies that were moving from one location into another. That purchase enabled me to keep in touch with my former customers, without violating my noncompete.

After a few years in that business, I discovered many companies didn't want to move everything they had accumulated to their new location, especially if they didn't really need those files or records anymore. Instead, they wanted to purge their offices before moving the items they really needed. I happened to be out on the golf course one day and one of the guys I was playing with mentioned that he owned a small shredding business, called Shred-X. He had only one truck, but I realized this was just what I needed for my customer base, so I bought his business then and there, on the greens.

Now I had another way to stay in touch with my customers without selling them office supplies. I approached all my former customers and offered them shredding, at less than they were paying somewhere else. Again, I asked to look at their bills, and when I saw, for example, that someone was paying twenty dollars per bin, I offered to charge them fifteen dollars per bin. Nobody cares who does their shredding, but since I had developed long-term relationships with all my customers, they were happy to give me that business if I could save them some money.

Within five years, we grew from $100,000 to $10 million by leveraging our customer base—with added value only with cost reductions. I added value to the shredding business by suggesting that my customers offer shredding to *their* customers. All they needed to do was tell their customers in advance that there would be free shredding in their parking lot, on a Saturday.

The trucks were empty on weekends anyway, and this was a great perk for our customers' employees and clients to come and shred whatever they wanted. This happened years before people bought their own low-cost shredders, so this provided a free service to the community, to our customers' customers.

Each truck could hold about eight thousand pounds of paper, and we sold the paper to recyclers for about $200 a ton, and made a profit of $800 per truck. But we weren't doing it for the money; we wanted to endear ourselves to our customers by creating added value. Moreover, we didn't have any competition for this service; there were no other stationers that were offering free shredding.

Some of my ideas were copycats of what another company was doing, and there's nothing wrong with that. As the old saying goes, "Imitation is the sincerest form of flattery," and I'll take a great idea anywhere I can find it!

For example, Staples started advertising school supplies in August and the beginning of September, and it did an enormous amount of business in those months. I knew that many of my customers would simply take whatever their kids needed for school from the office supplies they had already bought for their company. The owners went into their stock rooms and took pens and pencils, paper and notebooks, rulers and scissors, anything their kids needed. After all, they had bought these items already, so instead of going out and buying the same items for their kids' school supplies, they simply took them from their companies.

I pitched my customers on the idea that they could offer the same thing to their employees, so they wouldn't have to worry about shopping for school supplies, and we would offer the same price to the employees that we offered to the company owners on its supplies. We offered to take their employees' orders, and bill them directly, as long as they used a credit card.

That didn't result in a lot of additional business for us from the employees, but it did create an added value to the company owners. Some of my customers took me up on this offer, and some didn't. But for the companies that did, their employees were happy because they got the same discount that the office did, and they felt that their companies had gone out of their way to help their employees' families.

Our customers were happy because we had made their employees happy. And we were happy because our customers would remember this added-value service we had provided and were more likely to continue to do business with us for many years to come.

I was constantly trying to come up with new ways we could add value for my customers. I was open to doing whatever I could for them. We tried to fulfill any request. If we couldn't do it, we obviously didn't, but the times we said no were few and far between. As much as possible, we tried to accommodate our customers because we knew they could buy office supplies anywhere, and we wanted them to buy from us.

Some of the business owners we sold to were involved with different charities, and from time to time, someone would ask us if we could donate something that they could give away as a prize. We would either donate supplies or offer the winner the opportunity to come to our warehouse and take home anything they could carry. Or, if it was a children's charity, we would offer a few kids the opportunity to come and take whatever they needed for school supplies or craft projects. Our products were not very exciting, but that's what we sold, so that's what we could offer in terms of product donations.

Later on, I became an investor in Alex Toys, which made Slinky toys and stuffed animals. Because I was a shareholder and on the board of Alex Toys, I took the same concept that I had used at my company and offered an entrée to the Alex Toys warehouse, which had products more appealing to children than office supplies. I offered a day at the warehouse for a few children to come in and take home any toys they wanted—as many as they could carry—as a giveaway to the charity serving those children.

In one case, the owner of a major law firm in New York also supported one of the charities that I had provided toys to, and when he heard what I had done, he was so appreciative that he gave my company all his office-supplies business. People don't forget when you do things for them or for their charities. I have my own charities that I support personally, but I also believed in supporting my customers' charities if they asked. This was another way we differentiated ourselves from our competitors. It improved our relationships with long-time customers, and that opened doors to new relationships with companies who, in turn, became new customers.

The one-solution approach I mentioned at the beginning of this chapter became even easier to sell after September 11, 2001, because it was more difficult to make deliveries to office buildings, especially in New York City. Customers wanted to have fewer truck drivers and fewer deliveries, so they were more open to buying office supplies, janitorial supplies, promotional products, and printing from a single source. We offered better service, along with competitive pricing, which made life easier for customers while improving our business at the same time. We were increasing our average order size and simultaneously driving down our costs since we were making fewer but larger deliveries to each customer.

Once our customers became accustomed to placing a single order for everything they needed, we created budgets on their computer systems to let them see how much they were spending in each location or in each department. This enabled management to have better control, which was another value-added service we provided. Now they could track their costs, see who was buying what and how often they were buying it, which allowed our customers to better plan their expenditures. All we needed to do was convince them to try this approach, while reassuring them that we could be competitive in terms of pricing. As long as they got the price and the service when they wanted it, our customers were delighted.

## INCREASE YOUR BUSINESS BY EXPANDING YOUR PRODUCT LINE

One of the first big accounts I landed, in 1974 or so, was Herman's World of Sporting Goods, which had more than a hundred twenty-five stores, mostly in the Northeastern United States. Herman's was the first sporting goods superstore. When the company opened a new location, we received orders for furniture and everything they needed in the stores. That allowed us to expand into selling furniture and fixtures, as well as office supplies. That business grew enormously.

It was easy to start offering furniture to our customers because at that time it wasn't possible to buy furniture directly from a furniture manufacturer. There were furniture companies throughout the United States that bought from the manufacturers and created their own catalogs. Also, office furniture was very basic then. Companies typically bought metal desks (usually in one of only a few colors: brown, beige, or black) that had faux-walnut Formica top surfaces.

They also typically bought five-drawer filing cabinets and a few office chairs: an executive chair, a side chair for visitors, and a basic secretary's chair.

This was the standard practice before companies started creating "workspaces" and hired interior designers to buy from specialty furniture companies. We expanded into that area ourselves by hiring people to do the design work, then buying the furniture from the manufacturers and taking customers to the designers' showrooms. Before I sold my third business, we had eleven full-time designers on staff, and we sold close to $20 million a year in grade-A furniture, handled by one of our furniture designers. The typical job size in this aspect of the business was between $250,000 to $1.5 million.

One customer, a huge company in the communications industry, recently bought $1.2 million of workstations for a call center. They bought from us because we came up with a novel solution. The company had a bedbug problem and had to get rid of all its workstations. Instead of using cloth for our workstations, we used cork, which solved the bedbug problem. We got the business because we were always trying to think outside of the box and find creative solutions for our customers. We were problem solvers. We became more than a supplier; we became part of the solution, always trying to create added value.

Another of our customers bought $5 million in new furniture for a new headquarters just outside of New York City. When we first started selling furniture, all we needed to do was buy a furniture manufacturer's catalog and put our name on it. Our customers bought from the catalog, through us, and our wholesalers—either S.P. Richards or United—carried the actual merchandise. We were able to get it from the wholesalers within a day, and we could deliver it overnight.

As we grew, we developed relationships with manufacturers with more sophisticated lines of furniture, called "grade-A furniture." To sell these, we needed designers for our customers, and we supplied them at no charge. We knew when a customer was planning to move to a new location because our salespeople were friendly with the office managers. They would simply ask if they could have an opportunity to bid on furnishing the new location. Once we showed them there was no charge for the designer's time or work, I would say we signed about 70 percent of the projects we bid on. Most of the projects we didn't get were done by an architect's firm because they would call in their own designers whom they knew and had worked with before.

The furniture business took off immediately because we were selling simple desks and chairs. In the early 1970s, when Summit had about $300,000 in annual sales, we sold about $25,000 worth of chairs and desks and other basic furniture. Forty years later, in the last three years I was in business, we sold $40 million worth of furniture a year. Those sales included everything from customers who bought only one or two pieces of furniture, all the way up to customers who laid out entire offices, including design work, custom fabric, sometimes even rugs and curtains. Our designers could do everything. I'd say about half of that total—$20 million—came from sales of grade-A furniture.

Another benefit of this aspect of the business is that we didn't have to warehouse any furniture. Instead, we took our customers to showrooms, to give them an idea of what we could do for them. I did buy a few furniture dealers, at various times in my career, who had their own showrooms, and I did sell some grade-A furniture, but that wasn't a big part of my business. In the 1980s, I bought one company in Washington, D.C. that was doing $80 million a year, and $30 million to $40 million of that was sales of designed furniture. The company had a full staff and several showrooms devoted to many types of furniture, and it sold very large orders, of $1 million, $2 million, even $4 million each.

The furniture business is very cyclical. When the economy is booming, people are moving and redesigning and upgrading their offices. When business is lousy, nobody redesigns and people tend not to move; instead, they make do with what they have. Nevertheless, furniture was always part of our catalogs. At one point, we even produced our own catalog and sold pages to the manufacturers, which was a real money-maker for us. Furniture became a solid, profitable part of our business because we never had to carry an inch of inventory.

## OFFER SPECIALIZED SERVICES—
## WHATEVER YOUR CUSTOMERS NEED

Sometimes, we developed a specialized service for a customer. For example, our biggest client today is a public company, Tractor Supply Company (TSC). It was founded in the 1930s as a mail-order tractor-supply business, and has grown into a chain of retail stores that sells home-improvement products, lawn/garden/agriculture equipment supplies, and livestock and pet-care products. It was a customer of MYOP, which I bought in 2010, when Tractor Supply had seven or eight hundred stores. Today, the company has more than twice that many—nineteen hundred, and it continues to add stores. We sell TSC products it uses in its stores, not products that it resells. We also sell print services, office supplies, janitorial supplies, and anything else TSC uses for construction inside its stores.

The special service we provided for Tractor Supply was to create a weekly menu of all the products the company was featuring on sale. It was a very labor-intensive, manual process, and we only had three days to prepare it each week because the company needed to get it to the stores so they'd be ready to deliver from their warehouse.

We even sold them uniforms—usually shirts with the company's logo, which the employees wore. We had expanded into the uniform business for many of our customers, as another product-line extension, and we offered shirts, vests, aprons, hats, whatever a customer wanted or needed for its employees, usually with that customer's name or logo on the clothing.

We always pushed our fulfillment business. When we purchased MYOP in 2010, that put us on a new level because our largest account was Tractor Supply. We warehoused $1.6 million of Tractor Supply's inventory, and we billed them only when the company ordered for their seven to eight-hundred stores they had at the time.

Today, we warehouse more than $2.5 million and sell to more than nineteen-hundred stores. All the inventory we warehoused for Tractor Supply was guaranteed to be sold, and we became part of their company. We sat in on their expansion meetings, so we knew when they were opening new stores and if they were going to need new merchandise. We were part of the team, and we became ingrained as part of the company. Again, this created added value, which made us completely different from our competitors who didn't want to hold customers' inventory.

My salespeople also brought me ideas about how to add value to the service we were already providing to their customers. In one case, a salesman said one of his customers wanted us to carry store fixtures—shelving and other products used to display merchandise.

If it was a big enough contract, we considered it, analyzed it, and decided whether we could make money on this type of offering. For example, the Ralph Lauren Company was one of my customers at one time, and we carried custom fixtures for its stores that we normally didn't carry for other customers.

We also accommodated customers with special requests because we knew that if we went the extra mile by carrying products that we typically didn't sell—such as store fixtures—that was a way for us to get a new customer's entire account. If it was a big enough national account, we would do it because we knew that once we had the account, we would likely keep it forever, as long as we continued to provide great service at competitive prices.

Tractor Supply has been a customer for fifteen years: It was a customer of MYOP for seven years before I bought it in 2010, and we continued to give good service to Tractor Supply, who stayed with us. The company's managers renewed our contract every three years, instead of sending it out to bid because they were satisfied with us. On the other hand, we had to carry $2 million to $3 million worth of inventory for them in our warehouse, which was a big expense. We evaluated each situation individually. If we needed to take on additional expenses in order to create an added value for a particular customer, we'd do it as long as we thought it would pay off in the long run.

A further benefit arises when someone from one of our long-time customers takes a job at another company. As soon as the new people are settled in their new job, they often call us because they know we will give their new company the same great value-added service that we gave their previous company.

About a year and a half ago, the number two guy at Tractor Supply became the number one guy at A.C. Moore, the retail chain that sells arts-and-crafts supplies. At his new company, he was dealing with four or five different fulfillment houses instead of one. He called us and said, "This is right up your alley. We have five hundred stores. We're growing and expanding. We'd like you to take a look at the business and see if you can be competitive." He showed our people his company's costs because he didn't want to buy from four or five different companies. He wanted one-solution selling, one-stop shopping that we had provided to his previous employer.

We have all their business now.

Once you get a company's business, it finds more items that it's buying from other companies, which the customer is willing to give to you if you can be competitive. You don't need to be the cheapest; you just need to be competitive and offer a better solution. The deeper you can get into a customer's purchases, the harder it is to break that entanglement. Suppose there are two companies selling to one customer. One company is selling only xerographic paper and toner. The other company is selling that same customer its printed materials, promotional items, and janitorial supplies. Eventually, the company that is selling the customer more products for more money is going to make a pitch for the entire business. They're going to say, "I'm providing all this for you already, and I can save you money on your office supplies when you're buying from one person."

That's what we did at all three of my companies. We got our foot in the door however we could, and then we tried to open that door wider and wider. If we couldn't get in on office supplies, we'd go in on promotional products. If we couldn't get in that way, we'd try janitorial supplies. One way or another, we found a way in, then we leveraged what we did so well that were able to get more out of that account, and that allowed us to create a strong relationship with the customer and rid ourselves of our competition.

Another thing that benefited our business is that very few companies want to stock proprietary inventory in their own warehouses, as we did, because they had to lay out the money in advance. When the big guys came along—Staples and Office Depot—they didn't want that type of business. Since we knew that, we pitched that service whenever we bid on office supplies to a potential customer.

We also offered to create a website for our customers that would bear their names, so their employees would think they were ordering from their own company. We would handle all the fulfillment and deliveries the next day. That way, the customer wouldn't run out of inventory on items where they would otherwise have to pay rush charges to get them. And they wouldn't have to bother with delivering items to their various locations because we took care of that for them. That type of service went a long way with many of our customers.

## DIFFERENTIATE YOUR PRODUCTS BY ADDING VALUE AND OFFERING GREAT SERVICE:

1. *Be innovative about differentiating your business from your competitors.* It's increasingly difficult to compete with so many companies clamoring for your customers' dollars, so you need to be inventive.

2. *Find new ways to keep in touch with your customers.* Don't get complacent. Just because you have great customers now, don't take them for granted and expect that they'll continue to buy from you.

3. *Be the "go-to guy."* You can't compete solely on your products because products often become commodities; add value and go the extra mile so your customers won't want to do business with anyone else.

# SIX

# STAY ON TOP OF MARKET SHIFTS AND ALWAYS LOOK FOR NEW OPPORTUNITIES

*A*NOTHER WAY WE DIFFERENTIATED OURSELVES from our competitors was to expand what we offered in any way we could that made sense. It was another company's failure that led to one of our first and greatest successes—the coffee business. We didn't stop there, though. We also expanded the concept of office supplies to include many other products that offices use, such as bottled water, promotional products, janitorial and sanitation supplies, computer supplies, copiers and printers, shredding, and more.

## BE OPEN TO NEW PRODUCTS—EVEN IF THEY SEEM ANCILLARY

Back in 1994, my son, Michael, first brought the coffee-business idea to my management team and me. After he graduated from college, he bought into a company that sold coffee to businesses. Unfortunately, three months into running it, he discovered that the previous owners had been making fraudulent deals—which he obviously wanted no part of. We were able to get him out of that business with his integrity intact, but the real benefit was that he came to work with me in my businesses and brought his terrific idea.

He told us that we were missing the boat by not promoting coffee in the office to our customers. He believed the single-brewed cup of coffee was the future. He was so right, and that decision made us the first in the industry to offer coffee and beverages as a product class.

For those readers who are too young to remember, offices used to have a break room with an old-fashioned drip coffee pot. Obviously, as the day wore on, the coffee in that pot got staler and staler, so the market was ripe for the single-brewed cup, which office workers could make fresh when they wanted it, and in any of a variety of flavors.

Also, although coffee was offered in most office-supply catalogs, customers at that time didn't buy their coffee from office-supply companies. Instead, coffee was a separate business, serviced by other, non-office-supply companies that specialized in coffee, beverages, and snack foods.

We started with Flavia, made by the Mars candy company. The more customers we introduced it to, the more we sold. We were almost never turned down for a trial—after all, who doesn't want free coffee? And once a customer tried the product, that customer would keep the machine and order more machines for each floor of their business.

We also raffled off free coffee machines at vendor trade shows, such as the "Tabletop Show," which is held in New York every year at one of the major hotels. These were huge shows, and thousands of our customers came from New Jersey, New York, Westchester, and Connecticut. This was another terrific way to promote the coffee business. Once a company introduced the coffee machine to its employees, the demand for single-brewed cups surged. This is the same marketing model that Gillette used for razors: Once you sell people razors, they need to keep buying new razor blades. The same thing happened to us with coffee.

We launched this business at the beginning of the trend toward single cups of brewed coffee, and the gross profit was 50 percent, which is unheard-of in our industry! This became the most profitable piece of our business. In fact, when Office Depot purchased our company in 2006, it paid extra because of this single-brewed business we were in. By then, we had switched from Flavia to Keurig, and we were Keurig's largest customer, selling three million cups of coffee a month. We had built it into a $50 million division. At the same time, Office Depot wasn't selling any single brewed coffee. Today, Office Depot sells more than $500 million of coffee.

Also, we had almost no competition in the coffee business until we sold to Office Depot. Our largest independent competitor in the office-supply business was W.B. Mason, which didn't want to do anything in beverages or food. However, W.B. had to get into the coffee business when it hired a large group of our salespeople away from Office Depot. Those salespeople had been selling coffee to their customers, who would have changed vendors entirely if they couldn't obtain the same products and service from W.B. Mason that they had been receiving when they were buying from Office Depot. If I had to guess what that business is worth today, I estimate the company is doing about $100 million to $200 million in coffee alone. But our success was because of Michael's idea to get into the coffee business and expand into another vertical market.

Of course, we also expanded our beverage line because not everyone drinks coffee. Before we sold Allied to Office Depot, Keurig came out with tea, and Michael suggested sending a box of tea to each of our customers, again, as a free trial. Our customers tried it, and we immediately sold $1 million in tea over the next twelve months. That success was a direct result of our being proactive and on the lookout for new product opportunities that would be of interest and appealing to our customers. The one-solution idea was powerful: We went every day to our customers' locations, so why not provide them with one delivery, one bill, and fewer drivers walking through their spaces? Coffee became tea, sugar, spoons, cups, plates, etc.—all new products for us, as we expanded beyond coffee.

Building on the coffee and tea business, we then added bottled water. Many offices still had the traditional water cooler, but when bottled water started to become popular, companies started bringing in that, too. They can buy it for less money at stores like Costco, but companies don't do their purchasing there; they buy from companies like ours. After all, we were going into their offices to bring them office supplies, so bottled water was just another product they bought from us. It became one of the top ten items in the office supply business because so many offices had refrigerators and pantries, which they kept stocked with pretzels, potato chips, candy, cereal, and other snack foods for their employees. Although we didn't as yet offer those foods, bottled water became a huge part of our business.

## LISTEN TO YOUR VENDORS:
## THEY KNOW WHAT YOUR COMPETITORS ARE SELLING

Another opportunity that was brought to our attention was the janitorial supply business, "jan/san," for short. The VP of sales for one of our suppliers (United Stationers) told us we were missing the boat on this. They said, "Your competitors are doing a much bigger job. Because of your size, you should be doing a minimum of 10 to 15 percent of your volume in janitorial supplies." This was in 2011, after we bought MYOP.

Like coffee and beverages, jan/san supplies were in our catalogs, and occasionally we did get orders for products like toilet paper, tissues, paper towels, toilet-seat covers, and others. We also sold products and equipment used to clean bathrooms, including mops, buckets, and garbage cans. We had always sold trash cans—the plastic ones that everyone in an office has next to their desks—but once we got into jan/san, we needed the big garbage cans that are used in bathrooms for paper towels and other trash. We sold everything except the chemicals used for cleaning because they involve special handling.

We sold jan/san products when customers ordered them from our catalogs, but we didn't promote these products or warehouse them. Jan/san wasn't an area that our salesmen focused on, until it was brought to our attention that we could do more in this area. We increased jan/san from 1 to 2 percent of our business to 6 to 7 percent, which was a significant amount in 2014. In dollar terms, it was only about $300,000 or $400,000 per month, but by the time we sold HiTouch in 2018, we had grown it to $12 million to $13 million annually.

One of our customers was Englewood Hospital, which had about eighteen-hundred paper-towel dispensers that were made by

Georgia-Pacific. You might think all paper-towel dispensers are a standard size and can use the same rolls, but that's not so. Every company customizes them, which means customers have to buy the paper towels that fit that dispenser from the same company. The fact that you need to change dispensers if you want to change paper towels is a deterrent. Englewood Hospital decided to buy paper towels from Kimberly-Clark, and it was our responsibility to change the dispensers. Hospitals are a big part of our customer base for jan/san, and we might never have had that business if we hadn't listened to our suppliers and responded to this terrific market opportunity.

We also offered promotional products to our customers. This started with our printing business in the 1980s because my first company, Summit, was in New York City and in those days, there were printers on almost every corner. As a result, it was easy to get letterhead, invoices, and other business forms custom-printed for our customers. The printing business expanded beyond printing only on paper, and we started printing on sweatshirts, T-shirts, hats, work aprons, and other items.

Then the promotional product line extended further because our customers wanted inexpensive items they could give away to their customers, such as folders, pens, coffee mugs, umbrellas, tote bags, etc. At the time, our biggest customers for promotional items were banks, which gave away promotional products whenever they opened a new branch, and to new customers.

One of our customers was Hudson Bank, a major bank in New Jersey. We warehoused Hudson Bank's promotional lollipops, dog biscuits, pens and pencils with their name on them, umbrellas, golf balls, hats, and anything else they would give away at grand openings of new bank branches. That was a decent-sized part of our business.

Those products gave our salesmen another income stream, and they were easy to sell.

After the World Trade Center Towers were destroyed on September 11, 2001, business practices in cities really changed. People didn't want to buy from multiple suppliers because that required many different truck drivers delivering to their locations. That made business owners and managers anxious, and security procedures increased dramatically. Everyone who entered a building needed to present a photo identification card and sign in, which led to long lines of visitors in many of the high rise office buildings.

This happened not only in New York City and Washington, D.C., but in all the large cities across the United States, many of which we sold to, including Boston, Chicago, Los Angeles, San Francisco, and more. Many companies stopped stocking supplies onsite, and office supplies were delivered only when customers needed them.

Our competitors didn't want that type of business because they would need a large warehouse to store all those supplies. They also needed the financial wherewithal to carry their customers' inventories because most didn't pay for those supplies until they were delivered. Our people did give us purchase orders, which protected us in case the customers were to discontinue a particular item or if they didn't order as much of the product as it thought it would at the outset. We typically agreed to four inventory turns a year. If their stock moved slower than that, we sold their products back to them—at cost-plus-profit price, not at cost.

This was another way we differentiated ourselves from our competitors in the industry. No other medium-sized or small independent stationery business did this on the scale we did. If they offered it at all, it was in a very small way, in the tens of thousands of dollars, whereas we warehoused millions of dollars' worth of customers' nationwide inventory. Other independent stationers bought their products from wholesalers.

Meanwhile, our big-box competitors, Staples and Office Depot, simply didn't want to warehouse any customer's proprietary inventory, unless they really had to accommodate a large customer—and even then, they typically warehoused only small quantities of products.

I believe we were the first company to create the one-stop-shopping approach in our industry. Even Staples didn't expand into it until late in 2016, when Staples' CEO decided to diversify. Of course, it had the money to do that, so they bought a billion-dollar promotional products company. Today, Staples does $2 billion selling toilet paper, tissues, towels, and Windex. Staples realized it had a hundred thousand customers who were buying these products elsewhere, and it made sense for the company to sell them since it was shipping other supplies to its customers anyway. Moreover, the higher the average order size, the lower the freight expense is in proportion to the order.

We had one of the highest average-order sizes in the industry because we delivered such a wide range of products to customers. Typical orders included custom-printed products, promotional products, coffee, office supplies, and janitorial supplies. We strove to deliver five, ten, fifteen or more cartons of merchandise to each company, in one order, delivered by one truck. After 9/11, customers were much more willing to have one supplier. Our one-solution selling approach was preferable from a security point of view to having multiple suppliers delivering different products.

## CREATE NEW DIVISIONS TO HANDLE
## ANCILLARY PRODUCT LINES

In addition to the coffee supply business, my son, Michael, continued to look for new strategic opportunities for us to get into. Another great idea he had was that we should be selling computer hardware, software, and related supplies. This was a product line that didn't exist when I first got into the office-supply business. Although there were computers then, they were huge mainframes located in "the computer room." The personal computer wasn't widespread until the early 1980s. They created many obsolete or nearly obsolete office supplies, including typewriter ribbons and White-out. This is why it's so important to keep up with new technologies. If we were still selling IBM Selectric typewriters, which were ubiquitous in offices when I was starting out, we would have gone out of business long ago.

We expanded into monitors, keyboards, mice, cables, power strips, computer cleaning products, printers, toner, printer paper, shredders, shredder lubricant sheets, shredder waste bags, and more. And, because we sold printers, we started selling copiers, too.

We created a separate division for selling computer equipment and supplies, and it quickly became a $10 million part of our business. Even though we didn't make much money on individual items because there's not a big markup, the dollar value of these orders was much higher as the products were more expensive than basic office supplies. Plus, we typically sold in much greater quantities. Consider the difference between an order for twenty or thirty or forty printers and an order for ten rolls of Scotch tape for $1.10 each. If you make 25 percent on a one-dollar item, you're making twenty-five cents, but if you're selling a $500 item and you make 10 percent, you're still making fifty dollars.

Also, all of the computer equipment we sold was drop-shipped directly from the manufacturers. We didn't carry any computers or related equipment in-house, unless it was something that a major customer bought regularly from us in high volume. For example, one of our customers was Montefiore Hospital in New York City, which bought at least a thousand printers a year. We carried four different printers for them, and we always had six of each in the house, so they could get next-day delivery if they needed it.

That division quickly grew to $2 million just from our business with Montefiore. The fact that we provided computer supplies tied other customers to us, which prevented our competitors from taking them. When W.B. Mason tried to bid for the contract with one of our customers, they didn't stand a chance because they didn't do printing or warehousing and they didn't sell computers or coffee and beverages. If a customer wanted to stop doing business with us, they would have to negotiate five different contracts to five different suppliers. That was the beauty and benefit of offering the one-solution sell.

Another way we differentiated our company from our competitors was to create different names for each division that sold individual types of products. Staples didn't do that. Everything they sold was under the Staples name. That became a problem for them when a customer wanted to do a million-dollar (or even a half-million-dollar) renovation of its offices. They were not going to think of Staples because people think Staples is just a commodities store. People don't associate Staples with interior designers and CAD (computer-aided design) systems that can facilitate and plan an expensive renovation.

Staples is finally starting to address this problem. After they purchased my last company, they realized that selling grade-A furniture under its own brand didn't work for the architect community.

Therefore, in 2019, the company began rolling out new brand names for such product lines as grade-A furniture and computer supplies.

Years earlier, we had the same problem when we bought MYOP, and with HiTouch. Our traditional office-supply customers didn't associate us with renovations, so my son, Michael—who was clearly ahead of his time—came up with the idea of creating a separate name for each aspect of our business. We called our furniture branch "DesignWorks" to let our customers know we provided interior design and decorating services for offices and other workspaces.

We differentiated all our other businesses as well. The computer equipment and supplies business was called ITSimplify, and our printer services was MyOfficePrinterServices. Rentacrate provided an environmentally green alternative to cardboard moving boxes. Our shredding service was Shred-X. We offered specialized technology solutions for real estate professionals and facility managers under the name FacilitySolutions.

We bought a company that had a product line specifically for schools, called Unity Education Resources and Equipment. We kept that name to differentiate it. Unity offered library furniture, primarily tables and chairs, cafeteria seating, early childhood furniture sized for toddlers and kindergarteners, playground equipment, collaborative classroom furniture, and even curriculum support materials. This division catered to a different market from the typical office furniture market, and we needed to differentiate it so that customers knew we were capable of accommodating their specific needs in schools and libraries.

All these company names included "A HiTouch Company" to let people know each one was still part of the HiTouch umbrella. Customers continued to receive a single delivery—the key to the one-solution sell—and they knew they were buying from an expert in IT services and computer products.

In the early 1990s, when we first got into the coffee business, we decided to hire specialists for each product line to help salespeople in these solutions, and we called them champions. Coffee was so different from our traditional office supply business that we knew we needed an expert to help sell it. Michael was our first champion because he had managed that business and knew it well.

All these different product lines and services we offered enabled our salespeople to be more successful because they had more to offer customers than our competitors. If our salespeople couldn't get in the door to sell office supplies, they did it by selling coffee and beverages and then expanded into office supplies. That's really the only way you can survive and thrive in this business. Unless you sell something that has a patent, or is unique, and people can't live without it, you need to find more items that create added value and give you a leg up on your competition.

## BE OPEN TO WHAT YOUR CUSTOMERS WANT

Many of the new product lines or services that we expanded into came from our own people. I always encouraged our division heads to think of other items they could add to the "basket of goodies" that their salespeople offered our customers. Sometimes, however, our customers asked us to do more for them, and, if we could, we were always happy to accommodate them. Too many companies and entrepreneurs think only in terms of what they themselves are doing, and how they can sell more than their competitors. That's an inward focus, and it's not a good way to grow your business.

We started selling cash-register rolls because managers at Tractor Supply Company (TSC) told us they were buying these from another company, but TSC wanted us to provide them. Every year, TSC found more products we could sell to them, so they could eliminate additional suppliers. We even had a full-time person on TSC's staff who attended meetings to learn what else we could do for them.

We also took over some of their promotional advertising materials, which we had been trying to get into for some time. TSC had been working with an advertising firm, and they had given us some of this business, but we wanted more. Their managers told us they were very unhappy with that firm because it wasn't able to keep up with how fast TSC was growing. TSC was adding about a hundred seventy-five stores a year, and its stores were getting bigger. Every week, the company had different items on sale in the stores, and it produced a deck of advertising cards for the fifty or sixty items on sale that week.

TSC's managers decided to continue to use their advertising firm to create the decks and print them, but they asked us to distribute the decks to its nineteen-hundred-plus stores across the country. We had a location in Nashville, and TSC was in Nashville. This worked out very well for both our companies.

AS TSC added new stores, each one had an office and each store needed a desk, a chair, and a filing cabinet. We also handled their store openings, where we staged everything so the new store would be ready to open for business. Each opening cost about $5,000, and if we handled a hundred and fifty to a hundred and seventy-five new stores a year, we sold approximately $750,000. That's a lot of money! TSC was a $16 million account, and still growing.

Hudson News, whose stores are located primarily in airports and train stations, is another customer for whom we expanded the product line. They sell newspapers, magazines, books, snacks, and drinks for people on the go. We started out doing all their signage and sale items. When they started selling sandwiches and muffins, we asked them what they were doing for labels. Since we were doing their signs, we could obviously do their labels as well. They preferred having their stores order what they needed from a website we developed for the parent company, so that the individual store managers thought they were ordering directly from the Hudson News' website. The parent company didn't want to buy from another company, but we were able to ship more in a single delivery, which also reduced their freight costs. The Hudson News account started as a $100,000-a-year account and it has since grown to $1 million a year.

For the most part, I always tried to say yes to new opportunities, products, services, and markets. However, there were some market opportunities we turned down. When we first got into the jan/san business, many customers wanted us to handle the chemicals they used for cleaning. We said no to that because we would have needed special trucks that separate and compartmentalize the chemicals from the other products on the truck, and special insurance on those trucks to ensure safe handling of these chemicals.

The only time we agreed to handle chemicals was for very important customers, and only if we could drop-ship the chemicals directly from the manufacturer to the customer, without having to personally handle the chemicals. We tried to avoid doing anything with chemicals because of our concern about warehousing them and of potential problems, such as spillage and flammability.

Another product line we stayed away from was food. Since we sold coffee and beverages, some of our customers wanted us to also handle food items. However, most of the foods these customers wanted were highly perishable, such as fresh fruit and fresh milk every day. To fulfill those orders, we would have had to hire someone to buy those items every day and check the freshness dates to ensure that they were still good. We didn't want to worry about freshness.

We felt the same way about vending, since it was also food items. When our customers asked us to do vending for them, we simply told them it wasn't something we handled, and we recommended another firm they should contact. Once in a while, if it was a big enough order, or if a salesperson persuaded us to do it to prevent him from losing that customer's business, we found a way for a vending company to handle it while we billed the customer, so the customer would pay only one bill. We didn't make a lot of money on those arrangements, and it was a business we really didn't want to handle.

Still, it was rare that we said no to customers. In general, we tried to accommodate any request our customers had, even the weirdest ones, if we could. We wanted them to believe we were there for them, whenever they needed something.

We even thought about going into the travel business by creating a concierge service for customers who could book their plane tickets and all their travel arrangements through us. However, after looking into it, we decided it would be too difficult to staff because of the expertise and qualifications required. We ultimately passed on it because we didn't want to start a business we didn't think would be a good fit.

## DON'T GET STUCK IN THE PAST:
## KEEP UP WITH TRENDS AND TECHNOLOGY

Any successful business needs to keep up with changing market trends and new technologies. When I started in this industry, companies were still using carbon paper. Today, many people don't even know what that is. Typewriters were replaced by computers, printers, and toner. Toner is, today, the second-biggest item sold in office supplies. Technology has changed, and the office-supply business has changed with it. We were able to keep up with those changes for so long because we were close to our suppliers, our salespeople, and our customers. They kept us informed about what they needed as technology changed and some products and services became obsolete.

Similarly, if you wanted to deposit money in a bank ATM just a few years ago, you had to fill out a deposit slip and put it in an envelope. Banks decided to make that process simpler by replacing their ATMs with machines that could read the checks themselves. The same is true about writing checks, which is how most people and businesses paid their bills before the Internet. Now, most people and companies pay online, which eliminates the need for printed checks. Everything today is becoming more and more automated. If you fight that, you can't be in business. You need to adapt to changing technologies.

One of the accomplishments I'm most proud of is our e-commerce business. Selling on Amazon has been one of our biggest successes. When I bought MYOP in 2010, the company was selling about $7,000 a day through Amazon, who paid us once a week, in full. I insisted that we expand this business. Butch Johnson, one of our partners, developed a relationship with Amazon and our suppliers and found more products he could sell at better pricing and better cost to us as long as those products were sold via Amazon. We were able to reduce our costs because manufacturers realized if they didn't allow their products to be sold on Amazon, they would lose a big part of their business.

We also discussed selling on eBay and other companies selling products from third-party companies like ours. If we wanted to do that, we needed the right software. At the time, we were experiencing some financial difficulties, but in spite of that, I insisted that we pursue this business. I knew it would be about a million-dollar expense, and would require almost a year to get the software up and running. I also knew that meant other projects would have to go by the wayside, but I thought it was critical that we do this.

Butch is an analytical genius, able to calculate how much product we could sell the next day if we lowered the price on something by a penny. Soon, numbers began increasing. After we developed the software, we were able to sell much more.

I believe Butch's work in this market was a huge game-changer. We started to see the fruits of our labor already in 2019, and I know it will pay off even more in years to come. Without Butch's genius, creativity, vision, and fortitude, this would never have happened. He alone developed the relationships with Amazon, at every level.

## *STAY ON TOP OF ON MARKET SHIFTS AND ALWAYS LOOK FOR NEW OPPORTUNITIES:*

1. *Be open to new ideas.* Don't let your business get pigeon-holed; welcome and encourage people to suggest new products and services that you can add to your business. They may become your most successful products ever!

2. *Listen to your suppliers: They know what your competition is doing.* Welcome ideas from all sources because you never know what might lead to your future success.

3. *Think about your customers' needs, rather than your own products.* Even if an idea has nothing to do with your current products or services, be open to what else your customers want and how you can provide it.

4. *Get to know your customers better: The more you know, the more you can sell.* Find out what would make your customers' work easier, and then provide that product or service. You'll both benefit.

5. *Keep up with new technology and new ways of doing business.* Work is constantly evolving, so you need to, too. Be constantly vigilant about new markets and new ways of doing business—or you'll soon be out of business.

# SEVEN

# KNOW YOUR FINANCIALS: MAKE SURE YOU'RE PROFITABLE

*T*HE MOST IMPORTANT FACTOR IN HAVING A PROFITABLE business is hiring the right person to handle the financials. If you are the business owner but not a financial whiz, you need to have someone who is. Throughout my career, I had the right financial people. I didn't always start out with the best, but I knew how critical it was to have them, and I always insisted on getting the right people.

## KNOW THE BASIC MATH TO RUN YOUR BUSINESS

I learned this lesson the hard way, when I bought Summit in 1972. I bought a one-third interest to join the two older co-owners, Percy Snitzer and Al Goldrich, whom my father had introduced to me from our country club. Al had a brother who owned an accounting firm, and Percy and Al outsourced their bookkeeping and account- ing to him. Since I was just starting out in the office supply business, my new partners told me that for everything that cost one dollar, they simply divided that in half, added that to the cost, and sold those products for a dollar fifty. That's a 50 percent markup, which resulted in a 33-⅓ percent gross profit.

At the end of the first year, Percy, Al, and I went to meet with Al's brother to discuss how we were doing financially. Referring to me, Al's brother said, "The young man is to be commended. He's doing a great job. You guys were doing $300,000. You lost your two biggest accounts that each wrote $100,000, but Howard is at a run rate of more than $1 million by himself. That's the good news." Then he added, "The bad news is, your overhead is running at 34 percent." Obviously, if our overhead was 34 percent, and our markup was running at 33-⅓ percent, we were losing money. We were close to breaking even, but we couldn't stay in business by breaking even. We knew we needed to raise our prices.

When I first met them, Percy and Al were seventy-two and sixty-nine, respectively. By the time of this meeting, one year later, Percy was showing signs of senility. I'm seventy-three, and people are aging better than they did back in 1972, which is almost fifty years ago. Today, many people in their seventies and eighties continue to work, as long as they're physically healthy and mentally astute. Unfortunately, I was soon to find out how lacking in mental astuteness my partners were.

After the meeting with our accountant, I went home and thought about his recommendation that we raise our prices. The next morning, I went into the office and told my partners, "Guys, I have an easy solution. Instead of dividing the cost in half and adding it back for a 50 percent markup and a 33-⅓ percent gross profit, we simply have to multiply by 66-⅔ to give us a 40 percent gross profit. Then, with our overhead at 34 percent or even 35 percent, we will add five points to the bottom line."

They looked at me blankly. They had no idea what I was talking about. I asked them, "What did I say that was confusing?" And that's when they told me, "We don't know how to multiply."

I was stunned.

I thought about it and realized they had probably never gone to school. They were in their seventies in 1972, which means they were born in the early 1900s. Lots of people back then didn't have formal education. They sometimes went to work when they were still children, age ten or younger, and learned whatever they needed to get by, usually either as apprentices if they were lucky, or by what today we call on-the-job training. Both of these guys were salesmen, and one was a ladies' man who sold well because he smiled and flattered his female customers. He didn't always know what he was selling, but he knew how to sell.

So I thought about how I could help my two older partners figure out how to calculate prices that would work for our business. I said, "If you have a $100 item, and if there's a 10 percent overhead factor, your $100 item now costs you $110. So what would you sell it for?" One of them answered, "Half of 110 is 55; 110 plus 55 equals 165. I would sell that for $165."

I said, "That's a 39-½ percent gross profit; that's close enough to the 40 percent we need. From now on, just do what you always do, except you need to add in the 10 percent overhead. That means every price will be 10 percent higher than it was, and that will get us close to a 40 percent gross profit."

We called that a "C" price list, and we used it for the next fifteen years, long after the two original owners were gone. We always had an overhead factor, though it wasn't always 10 percent; sometimes, it was 4 percent, sometimes 5, 6, or 7 percent. We didn't tell our salespeople the true cost of our products because we knew if we did, they would be afraid to ask for higher prices. You need to know the financial details of your business, though. If you sell too cheaply, you can obviously go out of business.

I never considered going out of business. I had borrowed money from my father's bank, and there was no way I was going to default on that loan. I wanted my first business and all my later ones to succeed. It was crucial for me to have good financial information. And I knew this company had the potential, if I could just get past this tough situation. Unfortunately, I couldn't get rid of the two guys who didn't know how to multiply because they were my partners. Fortunately, I was soon able to buy them out.

## HIRE GOOD FINANCIAL PEOPLE TO HELP YOU

That's when I brought in Jay Baitler to be my right-hand man. Jay strengthened the inside, not financially, but operationally, while I concentrated on building the business on the outside. We were a small company, but we had a very strong bookkeeper, Bea Weber. When you're doing a hundred orders a day, which is not a lot of transactions, a bookkeeper is able to handle the books. It's a different story when you're doing eight to ten-thousand orders a day. With that kind of volume, a business needs a much larger and more sophisticated accounting staff.

My father had degrees in accounting and finance, but he had retired by the time I went into the office supply business. He spent six months of the year in Florida, and although we talked every day on the phone, he never got involved in the day-to-day aspects of my operation, or any part of my business. He was interested in what was happening in my company; he knew numbers, and he knew how to set up a T-bar that showed a company's assets and liabilities. I also knew how to do it, but I'm not an accountant.

He didn't know anyone he could recommend to me to handle my company's finances. And truthfully, I didn't want him to get involved, although if I had asked for help, I'm sure he would have helped me.

Also, when I first bought into Summit, the company was doing only about $300,000 a year. I don't think we had more than fifty orders a day back then. Over the years, I grew it into a much larger business, and as it grew, we staffed up. At first, we had only Bea (the bookkeeper). We brought in another person, and then another. Eventually, we had a strong controller, Natalie Meyers. She wasn't a CFO, but she did a good job for us.

I sold Summit in 1987 to Buhrmann-Tetterode, the Dutch company that wanted to expand into the U.S. market. By then, Summit was a $55 million company. When BT took it over, the Dutch managers insisted on bringing in another financial person. BT wanted to buy more U.S. companies, and it needed a much stronger finance department to handle the acquisitions.

By 1990, BT had bought 5 companies that, in total, were doing $250 million worth of business. As mentioned, BT asked me to stay on after I sold Summit to them, and I built up the division I was running for BT from $55 million to $500 million. As a result, the company as a whole was doing well over $1 billion. BT was handling all our financials. They opened a corporate headquarters in Chicago and hired a very strong CFO. We did have someone locally in finance who reported directly to me, but he also regularly rolled up to the corporate office in Chicago.

It's critical that accounting not be a second-class function in one's business. You need to have a strong, reliable CFO to monitor your financials and make sure you're staying profitable. The CFO is of equal importance to the CEO or the COO of the company. We were fortunate that BT brought in the right people.

I left BT in 1996, stayed out of the industry until my non-compete expired, then bought Allied in 1998. At the time, it was doing $30 million of business, with eighty employees, and a weak accounting office. I immediately staffed up to bring in a strong team in logistics, accounting, marketing, and information technology. I knew we would be acquiring several more companies and growing quickly. To accomplish this, I needed a strong foundation. This became especially critical after it took us so long to recover from the tragic events of September 11, 2001.

I called a very close friend, Jay Green, who helped me recruit a strong financial candidate. Previously, Jay had been CFO for Columbia Pictures, and before that he worked for Price Waterhouse. Jay introduced me to Tony Cavalieri, whom he thought would be a good CFO for us. Jay and I both interviewed Tony, and I hired him in the latter part of 2002. Tony proved to be an excellent CFO, and he built a phenomenal accounting and finance team. Because of his leadership, we had numbers available to us on a timely basis whenever we needed them.

## MAKE SURE YOU GET TIMELY FINANCIAL UPDATES

When I run a business, I can't be two, three, four, or five months behind in my financial reporting, which happened when I had the wrong people running the accounting department. It's absolutely critical to get timely numbers, and to know the numbers are accurate. If I don't have current financial information, or if my information isn't accurate, that can cause huge problems if I run into a headwind and need to make snap judgments.

It's better to know where I stand as soon as possible, instead of finding out six or seven months after we've acquired other companies or taken on new projects. Timing is of the essence because if I find out too late that something isn't working, the financial success of my business, and perhaps even its viability, are going to be severely affected.

We were fortunate to have Tony at Allied. He was a key employee who assembled a terrific team of people to work for him. He understood the importance of surrounding oneself with the right people, which is the key to success in any venture.

As I've done throughout my career, I asked many of the talented people who had worked with me at previous companies to join me in my new business. This included Tony. I wanted him to run our finance department, and he agreed. The one hitch was that the new company was headquartered in Nashville. Tony lived in New Jersey, and didn't like to travel. He thought he could manage it without having to relocate to Nashville or traveling back and forth, or he would manage the department by phone. Since he had done such a great job at Allied, I agreed to try this arrangement, but I believed it wouldn't work out.

When we bought MYOP, it was doing about $120 million in

annual sales. The finance department was run by a head controller, who was not able to handle or build the proper staff. He left the company shortly after I arrived. We brought in someone else, but he didn't work out either and I had to let him go. There were a few lower-level people who stayed on. In fact, one of them, Jennifer Smith, has done a very good job and, as of this writing, is still with the company, but there was no one who was able to take on the role of CFO. We needed someone strong on-site, especially since Tony was trying to manage the department from afar. Finding the right local person proved difficult.

Mike Palmer was our COO, and he had an accounting background, so he traveled to Nashville to review our payables and receivables, and to provide the financial reporting information we needed. It helped somewhat, but Mike was so busy with all he was trying to handle that he just wasn't able to do everything that a full-time, on-site finance person should do. As a result, the company suffered from a weak accounting team and had difficulty getting to the numbers we needed on a timely basis to run the company. Soon, we were four months behind in reconciling our books.

We knew we needed to find someone new, so we hired a headhunter in Nashville and found five possible candidates, whom I then interviewed along with John Frisk (President of MYOP), and Mike Palmer (the COO). We all agreed on the same candidate, who interviewed very well. He lived in Nashville, which was a big plus. His background was in transportation. He was a CFO for a logistics company that did trucking for Staples and others, which meant he was familiar with our industry. It was a unanimous decision; we thought this guy would be great.

He turned out to be terrible. He was all talk and no action. He was not a people person, he couldn't build the right team, and he didn't work well with women. We started getting into trouble with the banks because he kept missing deadlines.

Even worse, the banks wouldn't let me fire him because they were worried that bringing in someone new would involve a time-consuming learning curve. They didn't want me to make any changes to delay our operations any further, and neither did one of our largest investors.

He lasted a year and a half. We gave him four months to become acclimated, but he couldn't deliver anything he said he would. He couldn't even balance the books. It became a nightmare.

We brought in consultants from Bernstein & Company, an accounting company based in New York. It cost us about $400,000. They helped somewhat, but he still wasn't able to deliver the financial information we needed on a timely basis. He had issues every other month because he didn't put in the right systems, even after the consultants left. We talked to them and to our banks, and by that time, everyone agreed that he was the wrong guy and we let him go.

The point of all this is that these problems should never have arisen, and they wouldn't have if we'd had someone strong on-site from the outset. We needed Tony, our CFO, to be in Nashville at least three days a week in order to build the right staff. But Tony didn't want to travel to Nashville, so we relied on controllers there who reported to Tony over the phone. Unfortunately, that didn't work. Tony needed to be on-site so he could see what was happening and improve it. He needed to interview and hire the right people for this department. Without him in Nashville, we never got our financial department on track.

At the beginning of this book, I mentioned how strongly I feel about loyalty to my vendors, our customers, and our employees. I believe now that my loyalty to Tony caused me to have a blind spot. He was a great CFO for Allied, but his heart and mind just weren't in it for MYOP. Also, when I bought MYOP, he was seventy-two years old. He had been talking about retiring, but he was trying to buy more time until he was ready. Finally, when I couldn't tolerate the situation anymore, I told Tony, "I think we have to expedite your retirement plans because I need somebody in Nashville to do this job. I can't afford to pay both of you, and by your own admission, you won't go down there. You can't run a business in Nashville from Saddle Brook, New Jersey."

He admitted I was right and agreed to step down. That was three years after I bought MYOP. During that time, the company was growing, and I was acquiring more companies. The bigger we got, the worse our financial situation became. We really needed to make a drastic change.

As soon as I bought MYOP, I realized we had problems in the finance and accounting department in Nashville. It was a functioning company, and its strength was derived strictly from John Frisk, the President, and Butch Johnson, the Executive Vice President of Merchandising. Before I bought it, MYOP was owned by two venture capitalists who had brought in a professional CEO to run the company with the intention of dressing it up and selling it. MYOP had the sales volume I was looking for, but I also knew it didn't have the infrastructure to support the company in every department. All it had going for it was Butch and John, who were holding the company together.

Going in, I knew we had an uphill battle. On the other hand, buying MYOP enabled me to get back into the business after four years out of the industry. We immediately hired an outside consulting firm to handle our HR work and do our payroll. I had a friend from my temple who did this type of work, so we hired his company. When we brought in our own people to run these functions (working on staff, full-time), we found we were still paying people who no longer worked for MYOP, and we were still giving COBRA benefits to people after their extensions had expired. It amounted to $40,000, and I wasn't happy to discover these errors.

That's what happens when you don't have the right people in key positions. It costs you more to have inefficient people. I can go out and sell all day long, and I may think I'm achieving the profit margin I need. But unless I know what my numbers really are, and unless my gross profit is what I think it is, I may be losing money every day.

When you own a business, you need to worry about your profit margin. At Allied, when Tony was our CFO, we had strong accounting systems. Summit was a relatively small company that made it easier to get the information we needed on a timely basis. When we bought MYOP in 2010, we jumped overnight from nothing to $120 million. We had one employee in the finance department because when the company's investors decided to sell the business, in order to keep the overhead down, they fired everybody. The CEO that the investors put in place had brought in his finance expert to be CFO, until we bought the company, and the CEO and his CFO went back to their hedge funds.

## DON'T BE CHEAP:
## HIRE THE BEST FINANCIAL PEOPLE YOU CAN FIND

Since I've now retired from running my own business, I don't need to worry about financial machinations anymore, although I still advise other business owners so they may learn from my experiences. Glenn Popowitz, who owns Direct Supplies Warehouse, is about to double his business by opening a second warehouse in Baltimore. That's terrific, but the expansion means it's even more important to have the right people supporting him.

Right now, he doesn't have that. He has a controller on the inside, and an outside accountant who does his books. That might have been enough when Glenn's business was doing $25 million a year, but, as I told him, "When you get to $50 million, you're not a mom-and-pop company anymore. You need a strong COO, a strong CFO, and a strong IT manager." He was planning to hire additional salespeople, who would bring in an additional $20 million or so a year, but I advised him not to do that until he had those three key people. I told him, "Those are the essential three you need to build your business. If you don't have the right guys, and you don't spend the money, you can't go forward. You'll be out of business before you know it. Don't be cheap about it. Spend the money and get the best people you can."

The people working for Glenn in those positions just weren't cutting it. He had hired one of his neighbors to be his COO. The guy had lost his job, and he asked Glenn if he needed anybody to help out in the company, which was doing about $1.5 million a year. Shortly after Glenn bought the company, the person who had been running operations for the past forty years announced that he was retiring. As a result, Glenn did need someone to be his right-hand man. He hired his neighbor because he was in the right place at the right time, and it seemed they could help each other out, but it soon became apparent that his new COO wasn't strong enough to handle the position in this company, let alone Baltimore. There were obsolete products on the shelves, which makes no sense because that's not active inventory. It was getting in the way and occupying space that is needed for products that are being sold actively and need to be easily accessed.

Finally, because the warehouse was so disorganized and cluttered, Glenn himself had to go there before going to his office, and he helped pick orders to get them out the door and to the customers who had ordered them. Picking orders isn't Glenn's strength, and even if it were, that's not what the owner of a business should be doing. He's best at getting customers and selling, and that's what he needed to be spending his time doing, not working in the warehouse because the guy he hired to manage it couldn't do the job. That's why I always had a right-hand man to manage the inside of my businesses: Jay Baitler, Mike Palmer, and John Frisk. Because they were so strong in running our operation, they enabled me to do what I did best: Find customers and sell.

Glenn finally told this guy that he was going to hire a true COO. Glenn asked me to interview the new prospective hire after he had to provide a second opinion. We found a really strong person with outstanding experience. Time will tell.

Meanwhile, Glenn is trying to find another role in his company for his neighbor. He won't be making the same money, but he'll have a job, and he'll still be part of the team.

With his COO situation sorted out, I advised Glenn to find a new CFO, too. My recruiter friend Jay Green recommended someone who had many years of experience at one of the Big Four accounting firms, and Jay thought Glenn would benefit from working with someone more mature. I agreed to meet with him because of my friendship with Jay Green. After meeting him, I believed he could do the job because Glenn's business was relatively small. At the time, he was doing about $15 million to $16 million. I thought he would establish the necessary disciplines, set up a proper accounting department, and bring in the right staff to handle collections and payables.

Unfortunately, he didn't work out. He was good at numbers, but he wasn't a good enough leader, and he failed to set up the disciplines that were needed. After only six months on the job, he wasn't getting the numbers out fast enough. He was always three months behind in getting the financial information Glenn needed to run his business effectively. Also, the CFO never got the salesmen to follow the procedures necessary to track their sales. I know from experience that salesmen will run you ragged and will walk all over you if you let them. They're always more interested in getting the sale and fulfilling the orders to please their customers than in doing the paperwork that the accounting department needs.

When we talked to the CFO about this, he blamed everyone else, saying, "Your computer system is not doing this, the salesmen aren't putting in the tickets properly," and so forth. But we told him, "We gave you carte blanche. We told you to put the disciplines in. If the salesmen aren't doing their billing fast enough, or whatever else isn't happening, you were the one responsible to set all that up." But he didn't. Or he couldn't.

Once again, Glenn is looking for a CFO.

In the meantime, we're having his accountants come in twice a month, instead of once a month, to stay on top of things. Glenn hired more people to get the billing done faster and he is taking a physical inventory so we know for sure when there's a problem. He's doing the things that need to be done. I hope he will soon find an experienced CFO who will build the proper team.

The top financial person has to give you timely numbers that you can rely on because you need that information to make the right decisions about growing your business, hiring and firing people, giving raises and bonuses, and making sure you have the right staff. A knowledgeable, experienced, disciplined financial person is critical to success, and as your business grows, you're relying on him or her when you make business decisions.

You also need to build the right accounting team because you simply can't run a business unless they provide you with *timely* financial numbers, finish your bank reconciliations on time, and keep your balance sheet in order every month. If you can't get timely information, it's very hard to run a business—unless you're a single practitioner and you're simply billing and collecting revenue. Otherwise, the financials are critical. Unless you yourself are a whiz at this, you need to hire someone who is. Even if you are an expert in finance and accounting, you may not have time to devote to it, since you should be focusing on the bigger picture of growing your business.

My experiences with Summit, BT, Allied, and MYOP proved to be a key point about the financial side of these businesses. Success depends on your employees. You need to surround yourself with good people. That's why I strongly recommend that any entrepreneur going into business surround themselves with quality people, and, most importantly, a smart, disciplined financial expert.

## *KNOW YOUR FINANCIALS: MAKE SURE YOU'RE PROFITABLE:*

1. ***Don't think you can run a business with talented sales and marketing people only.*** You can't. You must have strong controls on the inside of your business, especially accounting.

2. ***Hire the right person to manage your financials and accounting.*** This is the most important hiring decision you'll make, so spend the time and money to hire right.

3. ***As your business grows, hire more sophisticated financial people.*** When you're running a small business, you can probably work with a bookkeeper and an outside accountant to manage your financials, but as your business grows, you'll need a controller and a CFO.

4. ***Make sure you're getting timely financial information.*** Insist that your financial people set up the right procedures to deliver timely information, and make sure they meet your deadlines, so you can make sound financial decisions.

# EIGHT

# LEARN HOW TO EVALUATE A BUSINESS YOU WANT TO BUY

*W*HEN YOU'RE CONSIDERING BUYING A BUSINESS, the key question is whether it's a strategic fit with your existing business. For example, suppose you're Ford Motors, and somebody came to you and said, "I have a phenomenal soda business for you to buy." You would turn that down, no matter how phenomenal the business was, because it so obviously doesn't fit in with car manufacturing. Of course, there are holding companies and venture capitalist firms that buy companies in different industries, but that's an entirely different business model from mine. Here's how I evaluated opportunities to buy businesses over the past forty years.

## DON'T MERGE; BUY OUT YOUR COMPETITORS

Right after I bought Summit, I bought a small competitor that was located a block away from me. We were located at 38 W. 26th Street, and this other business was at 38 W. 25th Street; the backs of our buildings touched each other. It was early 1974 when the owner of that business called me up one day and said, "You're a young guy. I'm a young guy. I'm in business with my father and my uncle. I know you have two elderly partners. I'd like to talk to you, and I wonder if we could meet."

A few days later, we met for breakfast at a nearby diner, The Spotlight. We sat down and ordered, and before our food even arrived, he said to me, "We should merge. Our businesses are about the same size. My father is dying, my uncle is going to retire, and I'm taking over the company. I'll be the sole owner of the company."

I knew I wanted to buy out my partners, and I've always been willing to consider any reasonable offer or idea, so I started asking the important questions. I asked what he thought his sales were, and he said, "One and a half," meaning $1.5 million a year. Then I asked what he thought his inventory was worth, and he said, "Two hundred and fifty thousand." So I said, "I'd like to see your operation."

Like Summit Office Supply, his was a first-floor business. He had a store front and a basement, where he kept his inventory. We walked over to his building, went downstairs into the basement, and as soon as he turned on the light and I looked around, I told him, "We just met, and I don't know you, but I know you don't have a dollar more than a hundred thousand dollars' worth of inventory here."

He asked why I would say that, and I said, "I can tell just by looking at what you have here. So before I'd even think about merging with you, we would have to take a physical inventory."

At this, he came clean, and said, "Well, to be honest, I think we have ninety-eight thousand in inventory. But if I report ninety-eight thousand to the bank, I'm going to lose seventy-five thousand worth of credit. I can't do that."

What he was referring to was the way banks lent money to small businesses like ours in those days. We both did accounts receivable financing, which meant we pledged our receivables to the bank, which would then lend eighty cents on the dollar. So when I sold, for example, a hundred dollar order, I would get eighty dollars in advance. On your inventory, a bank would lend fifty cents in advance. That was your line of credit, and that's how you got money. If you were growing, the more you sold, the more availability of cash you had, and the more inventory you had to buy. This guy had inflated the value of his inventory from $100,000 to $250,000 so that he could get a $125,000 line of credit from his bank. If he told the bank that the actual value of his inventory was only $100,000 (which it was), he would have lost $75,000 worth of credit on the $150,000 in inventory that he didn't really have.

I told him, "Your business is losing money. You're going bankrupt." I figured that's why he had called me, because he knew he was in trouble. Still, I was willing to consider buying his business, for several reasons. First, he was a very talented salesman. Second, he had a few other terrific salespeople that would come with him. Third, his location was so close to mine, so I could easily expand my business while getting rid of his building and the overhead that went with it. Finally, buying his company would be an easy way for me to grow my business. It was a springboard for growth.

I made him an offer, but not the offer he wanted or was expecting. I proposed that he meet with a bankruptcy attorney I knew, then we would meet with his creditors. Then, I offered him a job working for me, as a salesman. And if he and his salespeople could sell what he thought they could sell by the end of the year—which he estimated was $3 million—then I would give him 25 percent of the company.

We made a deal—not that day, but a few weeks later, after he had some time to think about what I had proposed. He accepted my offer because he had no choice. He really was going bankrupt. He couldn't run a business because he didn't know what he was doing on the inside, but he came to work for me, and he proved to be a great networker and a phenomenal salesman, maybe the best in the industry, at a very high gross profit.

The partnership didn't last long, but we made a new deal with him and his salespeople, where we created a win for him, a win for his salespeople, and a win for us

## FIND OUT *EVERYTHING* BEFORE YOU BUY A BUSINESS

The next company I bought was another small competitor in New York City, also around the corner from me. The owner came to me because he had two partners, one who was retiring and the other who was planning to retire soon. He heard I was growing, and he knew I had bought this other business. He wanted to merge with me, but he wanted 55 percent of the company. He felt that was justified because he was selling about $8 million a year, while I was selling $6 million. I told him, "But I make more money than you do, individually and corporately. My company's much more profitable than your company."

When I did my due diligence on his company, I found he was in the same situation that the other business I had just acquired had been in. He had overstated his inventory, and his receivables weren't collectible. He was flirting with bankruptcy. We met with his creditors and agreed that they would get paid one hundred cents on the dollar.

In 1980, we announced that we were going to become fully computerized. We told all our salespeople that our procedures would be changing and showed them how they would have to put their accounts on the books, and how all our products would be priced. The computers would track everything.

The day we made that announcement, the previous owner of the business quit. I knew he would because he would have to record everything through our business, and he would have to divulge what he was really doing. Until we started using computers, we never saw him. He delivered his products himself in his own vans, and he did his own billing. The computerized record-keeping would take all that away from him. So he went to work for another stationery business in New York.

I didn't mind losing him, even though he sold $5 million to $6 million a year. He was one of the best salesmen in the industry, but that didn't matter as much to me as having trustworthy people working for me.

Before he left, I told him he needed to make our business whole. He had gotten into the proprietary business for two of his largest accounts, and we had a large stock of inventory specific to those accounts. I told him he needed to take that out of our warehouse and pay the company the price at which we would have sold it, which was about $1 million. He said his new employer would buy it—but we didn't get that money until more than a year later, and it was a painful process to pursue the money he owed me.

People do not change their spots. As much as you think you can set up controls, once a salesperson is accustomed to selling a certain way and doesn't realize what he's doing may be dishonest, he's always going to look for the easy way out. Don't think you can change the world and that maybe you'll get lucky; it usually doesn't work.

In another company we were about to purchase in Baltimore, the numbers didn't make sense. The company's profit margin was simply too high, and we couldn't figure out why. Then I realized the owner wasn't paying sales tax, and that's how he was able to overstate his profits. So I met with the owner and told him he could go to jail for what he was doing, but if he still wanted me to purchase his company, he would have to go to the IRS, come clean, and pay back all the back taxes he owed. Then, I would be willing to offer a new price based on his corrected numbers.

The owner blamed his bookkeeper and said he was not aware of the tax problem. He said he wanted time to clean up his company, and we could revisit the sale a year later. A year later, we bought his company at a new agreed-upon number, which was much less than our original offer, of course. The lesson we learned was that you just can't be too careful at accepting the owner's numbers, even if they're audited.

## SPREAD THE WORD THAT YOU'RE OPEN TO BUYING BUSINESSES

After I bought my first few companies, I bought several other small ones in the area. One was in Westchester, and another on Long Island. I bought a small company in New Jersey that did about $1.5 million a year in sales. The owner had become ill and his son wanted to run the business, but he didn't have the ability to manage it. When his father died, his son came to work for me as a salesman. Then a friend asked me to look at his brother-in-law's business, in New York City. His father had also died, and he was losing the lease, so I bought that business too.

That's how my business grew. Most of these business owners came to me because they had some problem with their companies, and they heard I would make deals pretty fast. I looked at their stores, their operations, and their books, and I could easily see if there was synergy with my business. I made deals quickly and then, just as quickly, I integrated those companies into mine. We would meet with the buyer and try to finish the deal in less than a week, then the lawyers would take up to a month. We would need info on their company. Once we closed the deal, we integrated that business over the weekend. Teams came in and became Allied or HiTouch immediately. When we bought MYOP, because of the nuances in our IT requirements, the deals took up to ninety days to fully integrate.

Over the course of my career, I bought about forty businesses, and I estimate that in about 90 percent of the acquisitions, the owners approached me. They usually sold the most in their company, but they couldn't run a business on a day-to-day basis. Since we had more added value by selling more services, they saw an opportunity to sell more to their existing customer base. Therefore, by increasing their sales, they would make more money selling for me than they did owning their business. This was a win-win for both parties.

Buying most of these businesses was fast and easy because I was essentially buying them with their own money. If you make them settle with the bank, their assets are free and clear—their receivables and their inventory. If the seller has, say, $250,000 worth of inventory, $125,000 becomes available to me the day I buy the company. On an asset-based lending deal, most banks start off by giving you a minimum of 80 percent value on your outstanding receivables and 50 percent of the value of your inventory. If his annual sales were $2 million, and he had sixty days' worth of receivables outstanding, then he had about $320,000 of receivables, of which I received 80 percent, meaning $256,000. Add that to the $125,000 from the inventory, and I've got about $375,000. So, if I paid $250,000 in cash for this business, I netted $125,000 in cash right away.

That's how I bought many of these companies with their money, instead of my own. With the cost reductions in overhead and better cost of goods, it became instantly much more profitable and a very worthwhile deal to make.

Another company that contacted us was a business in Dallas. Although we were based in New Jersey and most of the first companies I bought were in New Jersey, New York, Connecticut, and other Northeastern states, we started to expand because many of our customers were companies that had offices all across the country. One of the strongest parts of my business was the legal profession, and we sold to some of the largest law firms in the United States.

We drop-shipped orders through a wholesaler in Dallas, and that business grew to $2 million a year. Soon enough, word spread that we were doing business in Texas, and I got a call from someone who said, "I hear you're interested in buying businesses. I'm in Dallas, I'm doing $8 million a year, and I'd like to sell my business."

We flew to Dallas to look at his company. I asked him what price he was looking for—I always recommend that someone interested in buying a business ask the seller what price he or she wants. I don't recommend making an offer before you know what the seller is looking for because if you start throwing out numbers, it's likely you're going to offer on the high side.

Keep in mind, though, that a seller is never going to give you a low number. Most business owners think their companies are magical and perfect. In this case, the Dallas business owner told me he was looking for $1 million. I said, "Based on what? What are you earning? I'm interested in buying your business, and I'm willing to sign an NDA. But I've got to be able to look at your books and see what you're making."

At that point, he told me his company was a lifestyle business. He was writing off expenses like his car, his wife's car, and other items on the books. I told him, "At the end of the day, you're making two hundred thousand. If I hire someone to run your business, I would pay him only a hundred thousand. You've got a hundred thousand in credit. What are you making on top of the hundred thousand?" He told me he didn't make anything on top of the $100,000, that he barely broke even. At that point, I thought, *This company is throwing off only $100,000, so what should I pay for this business? Four times, five times, maybe six times that.* But this guy was asking $1 million, which was ten times what he was making. That's not a good deal.

After I asked him what he did in the business, he said, "I pick inventory off the shelves. I pack it. I drive a truck sometimes when the driver doesn't come in. But usually I'm out selling. If you look at the business, of the eight million, I sell three million myself. Those are my accounts." I said, "If you're selling three million and you worked for me, you'd make two hundred thousand. I pay salesmen two hundred thousand on three million."

When he heard this, he said, "Wow. That's more than I make now."

Then I asked him how much he could sell if he didn't have to worry about driving the truck, and he didn't have to worry about buying merchandise, and he didn't have to worry about payroll. He told me he could sell another $1 million.

I told him, "If you sold four million, you would make three hundred thousand. But I'm not going to pay you a million dollars for your business. Your business is worth, at best, four to five hundred thousand dollars. Okay?"

Today, most businesses like his would sell for thirty cents on the dollar. That's why I walked him through all he was doing, what he was selling, and what he was earning—and how he could actually earn so much more if he were working for me. Not every business owner is cut out to run a business. Obviously, there's a lot to manage, and just because someone is a terrific salesman or a numbers whiz or an operations genius doesn't mean he or she can handle all the other aspects of running a business.

When we reviewed his operations and his books, it looked as though the business might be worth buying for $400,000. Before I agreed to buy it, I told him I wanted to see all his bills. I wanted to compare his wholesale prices with my wholesale prices. If, for example, there were a 10 percent savings on an $8 million business, at a 30 percent gross profit, that's $2.4 million. If he's buying $5.6 million of product, and if my costs from the wholesaler are 10 percent less, I would save at least $560,000 on purchasing.

Then I asked him about his employees because obviously there are duplicate functions that I can eliminate if I buy his business. He had a buyer; I had a buyer. He had an IT department; I had an IT department. He had accounting and finance people; I had accounting and finance people. In total, he had thirty employees. If I bought his business, I would let go at least eight of his employees because I had people who were already doing what his eight were doing. If those eight people each made $40,000, that's $320,000 I would save right off the bat. If each made $50,000, that's $400,000 I would save. Both savings would earn my company a minimum of $880,000.

That $400,000 that I offered to pay for his business would be a payback to our company in six months, which is an unbelievable deal.

That doesn't even take into consideration how I could grow that business after I acquired it. Most businesses I bought were selling only office supplies, whereas I was always looking to expand my product line. For example, that company wasn't selling coffee and beverages and when I asked him why not, he said, "We don't know how to sell coffee and beverages."

That's an easy fix: I sent our specialist down to Dallas, one week a month for the first three months, to show his salesmen how to sell these products. I figured we could increase his business right away from $8 million to $10 million, simply by adding the products that he wasn't already selling. And we did exactly that.

The most important thing to consider when buying companies is *synergy*. Everything is based on synergy—synergy of buying, synergy of products, and synergy of selling more to the existing customer base because we focused on the one-solution sell. Stick to what you know and do well already, and grow that type of business.

After we bought the company in Dallas, we decided we needed to grow in Texas. We called wholesalers and asked them to name the three best stationers to look at in Texas. Then I called each one of those recommendations and asked the owners, "Are you interested in selling your business? If so, we'd like to talk to you." So, we flew to Texas and made a deal in San Antonio and another one in Houston.

We did the same thing when we got into other markets. For example, after we bought a business in Washington, D.C., we looked at how we could get into Baltimore. Again, I called business owners and simply asked them if they were interested in or thinking about selling their businesses. Everybody in the industry knew who we were, and everybody knew we were buying companies, so when they got a call from us, they knew why we were calling. In a small business where the owner's son or son-in-law went into the business, the owner didn't sell it; he turned it over to the next generation. But if the owner was sixty or so, and if he had no heir to take it over, he sold to us. Most of the company owners wanted to work for another three or four years, so they cashed out and stayed on as salesmen after the sale. And they made more money working for me than they had made for themselves, with no headaches.

That's how we bought companies. We called it the "hub and spoke." Once we bought in a particular area, we set up a warehouse there. We closed the smaller warehouses that those companies were using, and we did cross-docking instead. With this system, our trucks went right to their docks, unloaded, and the goods were put directly on their own trucks.

This hub-and-spoke system also enabled us to buy more economically because we could stock 60 percent of the products we were buying, and they were buying 100 percent from the wholesaler. Our wholesale prices were 10 percent better than theirs, but our direct prices were 25 percent cheaper than they were buying from the wholesaler. This was a mix of benefits, all of which improved our bottom line.

## KNOW WHICH BUSINESSES YOU *SHOULDN'T* BUY

Of course, there were other companies we considered buying that we didn't buy. Some of them were companies that approached me because they were in trouble and they knew I bought businesses. Others were companies I wanted to buy, but the deal just didn't happen.

In most of those situations, the price was too high. The owners thought their businesses were worth more money than they really were. We couldn't make the numbers work. For example, in the last ten years of my career, I didn't want to buy any business that couldn't generate, on paper, a minimum of a 10 percent profit for the bottom line. That was our criterion.

All in all, I would say there were about seven to ten companies we bought over the years that met that criterion, and at least seven to ten others that we walked away from because the price was too high, or we couldn't get the synergy we wanted out of the deal, or sometimes the timing just wasn't right. There were times we were looking at more than one company, and during the due diligence, we learned that one was a much better buy than the other, and we could afford to buy only one.

One deal fell through because of a conflict over who would be in charge of a particular region of the country. Whenever I bought a company in a new area, I gave my word to the owner of that company that he or she would be the boss of any other company I bought later in the same region. It didn't matter if the later business was bigger or smaller. In one case, I bought a company in the D.C. area and made that same deal. However, the owner of the second company I wanted to buy said *he* wanted to be the boss and he didn't care that I had made a commitment to the owner of the first business in D.C. He said, "My business is bigger than his, and I'm a great salesman. I know I'll do more business than he will."

I reiterated that my word is my bond. If I give someone my word, I stand behind that. But he wouldn't budge. Then, I offered to ask the owner of the first company if he thought the second company was worth buying under those conditions and if he would consider taking a second position under the owner of the new company. He said, "No, you gave me your word." So, I walked away from the second deal. I wasn't going to renege on my word.

There was one business I really wanted to buy, but the deal didn't happen because the banks wouldn't lend me the money. We had gotten into the computer supply business, and we were selling MPS (managed print services). I heard about a company in Dallas that was selling about $6 million a year, with a high gross profit. Unfortunately, he wanted dollar for dollar for his business—in other words, $6 million. We didn't have the money to buy that business, and the payback would have taken four years, which didn't work for us.

Then we looked at another company in that same business, which also happened to be in Dallas. This company was owned by a husband-and-wife team, who sold MPS, computers, printers, and other hardware. They had started selling some office supplies, though this was a very small part of their business. It was a great company, I wanted to buy it, and they wanted to sell it. They sold about $18 million to $20 million in MPS alone. Their price was very high, but I saw the synergies.

We had a handshake agreement, but the sale didn't happen. I couldn't raise the money, and the banks weren't going to lend me any money to buy it then. They said it was too big of an acquisition, and the timing wasn't right because I had just bought another company. They felt I couldn't afford it, at least not then, so I had to walk away.

If I had to choose one company during my career that was "the one that got away," I think that business would be the one. Everything in life is timing. Six months earlier, I would have owned that company. The owners did everything they said they were going to do, and they doubled their business. Then they sold their company to one of the big-box stores.

I overpaid for only one company, Rentacrate. When I sold Allied to Office Depot in 2006, we were flush with money, and all my investors were happy. I had a noncompete that would keep me out of the business for four years, yet I wanted a way to stay in touch with my customers without violating my restrictive covenant so that I could come back into business in 2010, if I wanted to.

When I heard about Rentacrate, I was very impressed, for several reasons. First, the owner had almost a monopoly in this business because there was very little competition. Second, he had a product that provided a 50 percent gross profit. Third, his annual sales were about $24 million, and he was making about $4 million a year.

We paid him $24 million for his company. That was way too much to pay, but if I wanted to buy his company, I had to pay that price because he had three other buyers who were also interested. Again, everything is timing.

Then, right after we bought the company, we found there were things that he had hidden from us. One was that the gross profit was shrinking—from about 50 percent to about 30 percent. I could have sued him, but I didn't. Instead, he gave us 20 percent stock, meaning we paid him only 80 percent for his business, and he left the company. Four years later, I was about to go back in the office supply business, and I used the Rentacrate customers as my base; the company had served its purpose.

Eventually, I sold Rentacrate. The margins were down, and by this time, it was making only about $1 million a year, which was a significant drop from the $4 million a year that it had been doing when I bought it for $24 million. I sold it for $9 million. That was a good price, all things considered.

However, I'm not sure I'd make the same decision today. Even though it was somewhat different from my other businesses, it was an easy business to run. We sold to corporate America when they were moving their offices, and all of Rentacrate's customers were potential customers if I decided to go back into the office supply business when my restrictive covenant expired. There was no guarantee that I was going to go back four years later. We bought Rentacrate because we liked what we saw and we thought it was a business we could grow, but it never really grew because companies don't move often. Also, the movers started buying crates from us, so we were cannibalizing our own business in selling to them.

Fortunately, while we owned Rentacrate, we also went into the shredding business, which did become profitable. It was an offshoot of Rentacrate; we saw that businesses weren't moving as much stuff when they relocated. Instead, they were getting rid of it, by shredding it. When I bought Shred-X, the previous owner was doing $100,000 a year, and I grew that business to $10 million in only three years.

That also helped me leverage my accounts, when I came back as HiTouch in May 2010. We turned that $100,000 into $7.5 million of profit when we sold the Shred-X company in August 2016.

One final point I want to make about buying businesses is something I learned from my father: *Don't be a bottom fisher.* Remember the story I told in Chapter 1, where my father wanted to buy a company, and the owner wanted $1.2 million for it, but my father's partners refused to pay more than $1 million? They didn't make the deal, and that company went on to become incredibly successful. My father's partners realized their mistake and they never interfered again in how he handled his negotiations. My father believed that if a business is worth $1 million, it's worth $1.2 million, as long as the synergies are there.

I, too, learned the same lesson in my career: If someone else is bidding on the business, and you think the business is a worthwhile acquisition, don't be cheap. My father was proven right, on this point, many times.

## *LEARN HOW TO EVALUATE A BUSINESS YOU WANT TO BUY:*

1. ***Make sure the business you're thinking of buying is a good fit with the business you already own.*** If the new business is too different from the one you're already running (in products, customers, services, or vendors), it's unlikely to be successful, so walk away.

2. ***Don't make an offer until you know what the seller is looking for.*** Don't overpay; find out what's important to the seller, and then make an offer that will satisfy the seller and still be a good value for you.

3. ***Do your own due diligence.*** The seller has a vested interest in inflating the value of the company's sales, products, customers, and inventory, so assess the value yourself before making an offer.

4. ***Look at the books and other records.*** Sign an NDA if the seller wants you to, but make sure you review all the financials before making an offer; that's the only way to not get burned.

5. ***Estimate the costs you can save when acquiring a new business.*** You can eliminate salaries of people who handle the same functions as yours, and you should be able to buy at a higher discount or better terms as you acquire more companies and grow your business.

# NINE

# DECIDE WHEN TO SELL YOUR BUSINESS

*B*Y NOW, YOU KNOW THAT I EVENTUALLY SOLD all the businesses I bought and built up. I never really intended to have a business that I would pass down to future generations—although I did consider that, with one of my businesses, which I'll tell more about later in this chapter. It's possible that I sold because my father had sold all his businesses, so I had that experience as an example—but I had no interest in selling and then retiring young, as he did, at age fifty-four. I thoroughly enjoyed buying, building, improving, and managing my businesses, which is why I came back after selling my first two companies.

When I sold my third business at age seventy-three, it was finally time for me to step back and simply enjoy the fruits of all my labor over the years. The industry has changed and continues to change, and an independent dealer can't make it long-term in this industry. The cost of product differential, the technologies that must be kept up with, and the websites that have to be developed are all game changers. Customer loyalty is becoming passé; nowadays it's all about price, price, and price.

## CONSIDER THE FUTURE OF YOUR INDUSTRY

The first thing to keep in mind about selling a business is that the decision and the timing depend on the type of business you have. If your business is built on products that you have patented, then you have more control over when to sell. Your customers essentially have to come to you, since your products are unique. By contrast, if you're in a service business like my businesses were, you will get to a point where the industry will start to change and/or consolidate, which may foretell the end of your company.

For example, Amazon has not only changed the way consumers buy goods, but also how companies buy supplies. Buying online has had a dramatically negative effect on brick-and-mortar businesses. In my business, my competitors became not only the big-box stores like Staples and Office Depot but also Amazon, Walmart (after it bought e-commerce company Jet.com), and Costco. These companies have even replaced the office-supply superstores as the industry leaders, and they scared a lot of the smaller independent companies, which sold their businesses to companies like mine because we were willing and able to acquire businesses that were doing $3 million to $10 million in sales.

So, we started to see companies like Amazon competing in our industry and quickly controlling the websites and pricing. Then we saw technology changing how much paper and other products we were selling because those products either became obsolete or were used much more sparingly. Then we saw that even the big guys—Staples and Office Depot—were reporting that they weren't meeting their revenue goals for five, six, seven, even eight quarters in a row because of the new competition they were facing.

We also learned that some of our wholesalers (on whom we were totally dependent) were thinking of merging, and other wholesalers were being eliminated because of new competition from companies that previously didn't compete in our industry. Staples is making a run at the largest wholesaler in an industry where there are only two wholesalers supplying 80 percent or more of products to the majority of the independent dealers. This transaction is waiting for government approval, but at the time of this writing, all indications are that this deal will be happening any day.

Faced with all these challenges, we needed to ask ourselves what the future held for our business. We had to analyze the economic landscape and decide if it was time to plant seeds in the market-place that we were available for sale. You need to evaluate—even if your business is doing great, you're meeting your goals, and you have something unique—whether you would be willing to sell if you received the right offer.

I did exactly that with my first business—and the next two, as well. In 1986, after about fourteen years of building and running Summit Office Supply, my wife and I were invited to an industry event in Hawaii, organized by one of the big manufacturers of office supplies. We were invited to these events regularly, but I never went. Instead, I sent our management team, who appreciated and benefit-ted more from attending these events.

However, when we were invited in 1986, I said to my wife, "We're going to go to Hawaii, and I'm going to let it be known in various ways that I would entertain an offer if somebody wants to buy my company." I was a young hotshot in the industry, and I was growing very fast, but I also had pressure from the banks, and I knew what it was like to lose a big account, to see the economy turning, and to worry about recessions hitting. Building a business is an uphill battle. I was under pressure to put more money in the business on technology updates, on marketing, and in other investments to contribute to future growth.

For all these reasons and more, during this trip to Hawaii, I let it be known to the manufacturers who were there that I might be willing to sell my business, if the right offer came along. Manufacturers often got calls from companies where someone might say, "We're in a related business in Europe, and we're interested in buying a company in the United States; do you know any that would be worth buying?" If that happened, I was hoping one of the manufacturers who knew me might say something like, "Do you want the fastest-growing stationer and a young guy who knows the industry and can show you where to go? You should call Howard Brown. He might be available."

That's exactly what happened. A year later, I sold my business to a Dutch company, Buhrmann-Tetterode. I believe this happened because I had let people know I would be willing to sell if I received a good offer, and because of the timing. Arthur D. Little, the management consulting firm, had written a report on our industry, which had attracted the Dutch company's attention and piqued the interest of its managers. They came to the United States—*after* they had checked with some of the largest manufacturers in the industry.

BT's business was in a related industry. The company sold mostly printer paper and xerographic paper. BT wanted to get into another business, and it wanted to get into the United States, so it started

asking around. Since BT was not a direct competitor, the manufac-
turers were willing to suggest companies BT might consider buying.
And because I had put the word out that I might be willing to sell,
BT approached me and bought my first company.

My father had done the same thing when he was ready to sell his
companies. He put the word out. He let it be known that business
was great, but if the right offer came along, he would be willing to
consider it. In his case, he wanted to retire because he didn't enjoy
his work anymore, as it had become all internal meetings, rather
than meeting with customers. At heart, he was a salesman, and he
missed that interaction and problem-solving that he had experienced
earlier in his career. When the right offer came along, he was only
too happy to sell, a decision that allowed him to retire at fifty-four
and simply enjoy the rest of his life, which fortunately was another
thirty-three years.

I was only forty-two years old when I decided to sell Summit
Office Supply, and I certainly wasn't ready to stop working, but I
didn't consider what I would do next when I decided to sell. I very
much enjoyed running a business, but I also knew it was the right
time to sell this one. This wasn't a company I was going to turn over
to my children. In 1987, my son and daughter were still teenagers,
so they were nowhere near ready to take over the business, and none
of us had any idea what they would do after they finished school.

Still, if it hadn't been the right offer, I wouldn't have sold. Fortunately, BT was the right company to buy Summit, and BT asked
me to stay on to run my former company and the other companies
it would be acquiring in the United States. In fact, I would acquire
for them exclusively, which is what I did for the next nine years,
until 1996.

You have to read the tea leaves to know when it's time to sell your company. You have to know what the economy is doing, what your competitors are doing, how much product is being imported, and so forth. Business is cyclical—what goes up must come down, and vice versa. I was constantly reading tea leaves to keep an eye on how those cycles would affect my business. When there's an upturn in the economy, and employment is higher, then there are more people in the workforce. Also, in general, it's the smaller companies that hire more people and grow during an upturn, and those companies were our market.

Conversely, when there's a recession, people get laid off, and companies cut back on their spending. In a downturn, the furniture business is simply gone because companies don't spend to move or to redecorate their workspaces. If a chair is a little worn, for example, they'll simply wait for it to break before replacing it.

In the mid-1980s, in our industry, the ups started to move into the down cycle. I believed we would find a way out, but I also saw that the future was not going to be the same because there was new competition coming. In 1986, Staples and Office Depot came in as superstores and both started buying the biggest stationers out there, so we now faced new competitors with plenty of money.

## DON'T GET LULLED BY PAST SUCCESS

When business is good, it's easy to get lulled into thinking next year's business will be even better, but you can't let that happen. You need to be a little wary of success because the outlook can start to change, and you may be caught unawares if you're not constantly on the lookout.

In my career, there were many times when we got beat up. Even though we saw light at the end of the tunnel, we still decided that the pressure from our banks and customers was so great that if the right offer came up, we would sell our business. And that's exactly what happened in 1987, when I sold Summit.

I sold my second company, Allied, for the same reason. I built it up during the eight years I owned it (1998–2006), but many businesses were hit hard after September 11, 2001. In addition to the tremendous loss of life—including some of our own customers—we lost $11 million in receivables and another $20 million in business because it was impossible to make deliveries below 14th Street in New York City for many months after. We worked hard for the next several years, trying to recover from that disaster.

Finally, at the end of 2003, the banks we had loans with—Crédit Agricole, Société Générale, and Barclays, all foreign—wanted out, so much so that they were willing to take a major haircut on what we owed them. Since the United States was in the midst of the Gulf War, many foreign banks decided to sell off their portfolios, and our company was included in that. As a result, we were able to buy back the company. It was a huge risk and we had to find the money to finance the buyback, but we did it. We were able to go to GE Capital for an asset-based deal.

Then, in 2006, we knew that both Office Depot and Staples were in the market to buy smaller companies. I knew Office Depot would consider buying Allied because they were not in the coffee business, and more importantly, they were weakest in the Northeast. We could solve both of Office Depot's problems because we were doing $275 million in the Northeast, and we were the largest seller (among companies in the office-products industry) of coffee and beverages in the United States. In addition, our customer base in the Northeast included some of the finest law firms in the country, thus providing Office Depot with additional business throughout the United States and Europe, where many of these firms also conducted business. In fact, *Crain's* had just recently run an article stating that we served forty-nine of the fifty largest law firms in Washington, D.C.

Therefore, if Office Depot bought us, that would be a synergistic purchase, where it could leverage our sales and what was unique about our company. One of the members of my country club in New Jersey worked for a firm that represented Office Depot, so when I played golf with him, I mentioned that, indirectly. I said things like, "We are just cleaning Office Depot's clock. Their stores are so weak in the Northeast, and I can't believe they're not in the coffee business. We're the largest seller of coffee to companies." I planted these seeds in his mind, so if Office Depot's top managers started looking to buy a company, my country-club friend might mention us to them.

I believe that's what happened because we got a call from Office Depot, which led to us selling Allied in 2006. We opened up many new markets for Office Depot.

By this time, my son, Michael, was very much a part of Allied's business and success. He had joined me in the business in 1998, working in various capacities, and he'd become president in 2001. He didn't want me to sell the business because he wanted a chance to run it himself, especially since we had worked so hard to build it back up, and we had finally come back from all the problems of the previous few years. However, I knew it was time to sell for all of the reasons mentioned previously.

Fortunately, once Michael realized that selling was the right decision, he pushed to get a much higher price from what Office Depot originally offered. He said, "You're selling too cheap!," and pushed to get an extra $35 million, which we got.

## LOOK FOR THE RIGHT BUYER

When I decided I wanted to sell my company, I followed the same principles that I had used when selling my products to customers. You need to know your audience and then sell to that audience. You have to find out who is the right person to talk to, just like you need to find the right person to sell to when you're selling products. You want to plant the right seeds in the right places.

Fortunately, if you're interested in selling to a public company, you can find out more about the company by listening in on their calls with analysts and shareholders. Anybody can listen in on those calls, and you can often learn what the company's weaknesses are. A company might say something like, "We need to get deeper penetration into our account base. We need to offer more services." You can even drop hints as to how you can solve those weaknesses, especially to the company that represents them and is looking for possible acquisitions. Of course, you have to be able to find the right person at that company, too, so that when you're dropping those hints, they're not falling on deaf ears. Our competitors didn't have anything like our one-solution sell, and they were intrigued by it.

As a result, when Office Depot said, "Find me someone to buy," we were number one on the list. Then when Office Depot came to us, rather than us going to them, we asked for a ridiculous price. And we got it. So, the time to sell is when you see the market and the competitive landscape changing, and you're in a strong position. The highest the industry paid was thirty to thirty-five times sales or eight times EBITDA, yet the price at which we sold must have been one of the highest in the industry ever recorded as a multiple of sales. We got twelve times our forward earnings! That was unheard of for a commodity business. After all, we weren't selling something unique that we had invented.

Again, we were fortunate because the timing was right. Office Depot needed to get better traction in the Northeast. It needed to build a customer base in law firms, and it was not in the coffee and beverage business. Allied met all those needs, so all of that played a major role. In addition, Office Depot was eager to buy a major company and make an investment. We were in the right place at the right time.

Unfortunately, sometimes you don't have the luxury of selling when the time is right. Sometimes, you realize you need to sell because things are changing. As mentioned, you need to keep your pulse on your business and on the economy, and there will be times when you see that the economy is changing and you need to get out while you can.

For example, you might see that we're headed for a deep recession, which means that companies are going to start laying off employees. Fewer people working means fewer people drinking coffee and fewer people using office supplies at work. Higher unemployment is obviously bad for business. That's the opposite of a situation when business is good and your customers simply call and tell you, "I just hired twenty more people, so I need twenty more desks, twenty more chairs, and lots of other supplies stuff."

Also, it's not only recessions that decrease the volume of your business. Years ago, when companies started downsizing their on-site staff and allowed some or all of their employees to work from home and telecommute, that trend had an enormously negative effect on business-to-business office-supply sales. As that trend became more and more popular, fewer people were coming into the office, which again translated into lower coffee and beverage consumption and fewer pens and pencils needed. In addition, many companies started giving their at-home employees credit cards so that they could simply go to their local Staples or Office Depot and buy the supplies they needed to work.

That was when the office-supply business really started to shrink, and Staples and Office Depot started closing or downsizing some of their stores. And even the stores that remained open weren't as fully stocked anymore. Staples and Office Depot both missed twelve quarters in sales from 2014 to 2017. Both companies are getting out of Europe and trying to get into the added-value proposition.

I saw the writing on the wall, but when I tried to sell my third company, HiTouch, I was in a weak position. The people who were running Staples at that time knew HiTouch was in trouble financially. They negotiated with us, seemingly in good faith, but when it came time to finalize the deal, they lowered the price substantially. They thought we had no choice but to sell, and therefore we would be forced to accept their offer even though it was much lower than what we had originally agreed upon. But we weren't that desperate, and we walked away.

Six months later, they came back and offered a much lower price—almost half of their initial offer: $60 million instead of the original $110 million. They justified this low-ball offer because they said they didn't want our e-commerce business, which was about $30 million, and they didn't want our government business, which amounted to about $25 million. I told them I was confused because our government business was to VA hospitals, which they also sold to. When they heard that, they said they certainly did want that business.

I also told them our e-commerce business had grown substantially since their initial offer. In fact, by that time, we were the industry leader in e-commerce. So we negotiated a new deal with Staples—for $86 million.

However, at the closing, Staples tried to change the terms of the deal, so we walked away again.

Then in 2017, Staples was acquired by a private equity firm, Sycamore Partners. Shortly after that sale, the new managers realized that the company needed to buy other, smaller companies, in order to grow. When they learned about the two failed deals between Staples and HiTouch, they wanted to know why neither deal had been completed. After all, we were the second-largest independent stationer, after W.B. Mason, which was four times our size, but W.B. Mason wasn't interested in selling its company, didn't offer the added value, and certainly was not involved in the one-solution sell. W.B. Mason was just a plain bread-and-butter office-products company.

Sycamore took away the decision-making authority from the people we had been negotiating with at Staples before Sycamore acquired Staples. The Sycamore people met with us directly, so they would hear for themselves why the deals had fallen apart. When we met with them and told them about our e-commerce business, our one-solution approach to customers, and all the things we did, they said, "We want to buy your business." We told them, "We're not going through this again." They were persistent, though, and they told us they would close in thirty days. They said, "We're not going to make you go through what you went through before. We're making the decisions now."

Sycamore's managers saw the value of our Amazon business, our fulfillment business, and our customer service—so much so that they didn't even change our company's name after they bought us. In the past, Staples had always changed the names of the companies it acquired. But when Sycamore/Staples acquired my third company, it kept our name and simply added the Staples name. The name of the company is now HiTouch, Powered by Staples

Two months after Sycamore/Staples bought us, the two executives who had been running Staples were no longer running the company. They were demoted, and soon after that, they were fired! These were the people who had botched the first two deals Staples tried to make with HiTouch. They were fired for two main reasons. First, they were arrogant and they thought that because they worked for Staples—one of the leaders in the industry—they could renege on the deal they had made with my company. Second, they didn't have the vision and they didn't see what the new people from Sycamore saw.

Sycamore's people were also smart in bringing in a new CEO for Staples when they hired the president of Coca-Cola North America. Because he came from outside our industry, he also had a much different viewpoint and vision. He saw what HiTouch would bring to the table, and how it would add value to the rest of the Sycamore/Staples organization.

That's the benefit of selling your company to a synergistic buyer. He knows what overhead he can take out of your company, and what his purchasing power is. He's buying your company at what may be a decent price for you, but is nothing for him, because he can make his investment back in less than two years and have all your added value plus your offerings that he doesn't sell. He also sees that you will put him in businesses that he's not currently in. He can see the opportunity.

That's what happened when Sycamore/Staples acquired HiTouch. They had the vision, so it was an easier deal to make, and it worked out for both our companies. It was a win-win.

One last point I want to make about that sale—timing is every-thing in life, and that credo proved true once again when Sycamore/Staples bought HiTouch. Right after we sold, we learned that Syc-amore/Staples planned to buy the largest wholesaler in the indus-try: Essendant, a $7.5 billion company. The deal went through in September 2018, which was a year after Sycamore/Staples bought HiTouch, and it was conditionally approved by the Federal Trade Commission on January 31, 2019.

The acquisition of Essendant is going to change the office-supply industry tremendously because Staples had previously planned to buy a dozen other stationers. However, after they bought HiTouch, Staples stopped acquiring any other small stationers because they no longer needed to. All the small stationers in the United States bought their products from Essendant, so why would Staples buy those small companies if it now owned the company that was the wholesaler supplying those companies?

We were lucky that Sycamore/Staples bought us before buying Essendant because they probably wouldn't have bought my com-pany if the two deals had been reversed.

If I had still wanted to sell HiTouch, and Sycamore/Staples hadn't bought it, we would have kept fighting to survive in a dramatically changing industry and marketplace. Eventually, if I still wanted to sell the business, I would have had to hire a firm to represent me and try to peddle my company to another industry (i.e., *not* synergistic) buyer as an add-on to another company's business.

That would have been much harder, and I'm sure I would have had to sell for a much lower price. We kept pumping money into the business, and I had cut my salary to a third of what it was.

## DECIDE WHEN THE TIME IS RIGHT FOR *YOU* TO SELL

As a reminder, I was forty-two years old when I sold my first business, sixty-one when I sold my second business, but almost seventy-three when I sold my third business. There's a big difference in how I felt about each business because of what stage of life I was in. I started in business, with my first company, at age twenty-seven. I was married and had two children already by then, but if I didn't take a chance at that time, when would I? Even at age forty-two, I still had my whole life ahead of me, so I was confident I would recover any money I might lose.

By contrast, at seventy-three, I knew I didn't have much recovery time to get the money I would need to keep going forward. That's why I pushed so hard to find a sale, or a merger—something that would allow me to finish my long career on a high note. It was an uphill battle. We were always under-capitalized. In today's environment, money is king, and weak balances do not help for success.

I give this same advice to younger business owners: Build your business to the point that a larger company is going to see that it's worthwhile acquiring your company. If you're too small, your company won't be worth the effort involved in the acquisition because the process can be arduous and time-consuming.

On the other hand, if you enjoy what you're doing, and you don't need to cash out, you might not care about selling your business. For example, maybe you have a family business, with plenty of money in it. Maybe you sell a product that people need, or you have customers that you've been doing business with for many years and you've developed good, reliable relationships. Maybe you don't see any competition that is going to hurt you in any way. If all these factors are present and you're making a fortune, you might say, "Why should I give all this up?"

For instance, I have a close friend in the freight-forwarding business, and he is a major player in Canada, where he lives. He has built a business and trained his junior partners such that they are running the day-to-day aspects of the business, under his guidance. The company is so successful that it currently doesn't make sense to sell it. It has no products and no inventory, but it has service and well-established relationships that it has had for thirty years. The company is well capitalized, so why sell?

Your company can become a lifestyle business, and you can continue to run it until you decide to retire. Many of the companies I acquired were lifestyle businesses and many of those business owners made more money working for me as salesmen than they did when they owned their own companies.

However, I also caution business owners to not wait too long to consider selling their companies. Many people think they have all the time in the world to do everything they want to do in their lives, so they put off retiring. That doesn't always work out because you never know what will happen to you. How long do you want to wait to enjoy your life?

Also, if there's nothing unique about your business, you need to keep a close eye out for the right time to sell. As I've said throughout this book, there's nothing unique about the products my companies sold: pens, pencils, paper, and so forth. What *was* unique was how I added value to those products, so that customers wanted to buy from me. You need to keep coming up with new ideas for how to create more and more added value. For example, when I went into the coffee and beverage business, the margins were 50 percent gross profit. Today, however, you would be lucky to get 10 percent gross profit because that's become just another commodity.

Finally, you should always be willing to listen to anyone who expresses interest in buying your business—even if you're not at all ready to sell. You have to find out what the deal is. I never stopped listening because I've always thought it was important to find out what the value of my company was, at that time, even if it wasn't for sale. I took every call from people who said they wanted to talk to me about potentially buying my company. I got calls all the time, at least once a year. Some years, I received half a dozen calls. You've got to listen and keep your ears open to what's going on around you in the industry and in the economy.

There were even times when someone called me to discuss buying my company, when I realized it made more sense if I bought *his* company. In one case, my revenues were twice what the other company's were: I was doing $400 million, while he was doing only $200 million. Those deals never happened because the owner's ego usually got in the way, but I always learned something from everyone I met with during those conversations.

For example, one company owner I met with told me he had negotiated for better UPS rates. That had never occurred to me because that had never been such a big item. Then when we got into the e-commerce business, we started running up $8 million to $10 million a year in freight costs. If we could negotiate better rates—for instance, 10 percent less—that would save us at least $800,000. That's a lot of money! As a result, rates became more important, and I tucked that idea away in the back of my mind.

In short, you need to have an open mind. Keep an eye on what's happening in the industry and the marketplace. Be willing to meet with people who may be interested in buying your business. I was always a listener and a watcher, and that served me well to know when the time was right to sell my businesses. All of them.

## *DECIDE WHEN TO SELL YOUR BUSINESS:*

1. ***Think about the future of your business.*** It's all too easy to get caught up in the day-to-day challenges of running a company, but you need to keep an eye on how your competitors are doing, how the economy is doing, and how the industry as a whole is changing.

2. ***Consider where you are in your career and life.*** If you're still young, you still have years to recover if this business fails, but if you'd like to retire sooner rather than later, keep your ears open for opportunities to sell.

3. ***Always be willing to discuss selling.*** Even when you're not interested in selling, it's worthwhile to hear what someone else thinks your company is worth, and you might even pick up new ideas for how to run your business better while you still own it.

4. ***Put the word out that you might be willing to sell if the right offer came along.*** That doesn't mean you have to sell, but you want your company's name to be mentioned to other companies that may be looking to buy.

# CONCLUSION

IF YOU'VE READ THIS FAR, I'M CONFIDENT YOU'VE absorbed many of the lessons I learned in my fifty-year career. I'm fortunate that I've been successful in all my businesses—and in my life with my wife, children, and grandchildren. I've written this book to help people who want to create their own success, so here are a few final words of advice.

Learn as much as you can about business in general before going into business for yourself. Ask your family, friends, teachers, and any successful businesspeople you know or can arrange to meet if you can shadow them at work, sit in (silently) at their meetings, and ask them questions about how they conduct their businesses. Find good mentors (even if they don't know they're mentoring you), and soak up as much information as you can.

Be passionate about your business, even if it's not something you thought you could be passionate about. I'm not saying, "Do what you love, and the money will follow"; that's not feasible for everyone. But you *do* have to talk enthusiastically about your business, so that people will want to do business with you.

Look for customers *everywhere*. Start with the people you know. Then get to know more people, and talk about your business whenever you can. If you show that you enjoy what you do, people will respond, and you'll find it easy to grow your business and find new customers. Don't be afraid to ask for someone's business; if they're not interested or not in the market for what you do, that's okay. But if you don't ask for it, you probably wont get it.

Say yes whenever you can to customers, then figure out how to deliver what you've promised. Don't say no, as so many businesspeople do. Although it's easier to say no, you won't be able to grow your business that way. Instead, you need to be resourceful and innovative and deliver great customer service. When you do that, your customers will remember you and continue to buy from you, even if they can get a lower price somewhere else, because a buying decision isn't always about price. Customers are impressed by excellent service, and they'll keep coming back for more.

Find out what's really important to anyone you're negotiating with—whether a customer or a vendor. When you look at the transaction or deal from the other person's perspective, you gain an advantage and can usually deliver a result that will make you both happy.

Hire the best people you can. Some business owners are tyrants who want only weak people working for them so they can feel superior to their employees. That's not a good way to run a business. When you hire people who are smart, experienced, skilled, and talented, *everyone* succeeds. As the old saying goes, "A rising tide lifts all boats."

Get to know your employees, your customers, and your vendors. Find out what's important to them, offer to help them if you can, and be loyal to them so they'll be loyal to you. That loyalty will pay off in so many ways, not the least of which is financial. Develop long-term relationships that will last for years after your first encounter or transaction with someone.

Try to differentiate your business from your competition. Many businesses sell products or services that are essentially commodities, and even if you think what you do is unique, it isn't. There's always going to be someone else who finds a way to do something faster, smarter, or better. Don't be daunted by that prospect; just do what you can to offer *something more* to your customers, so that they will want to continue to do business with you.

Be open to new ideas for new products or new services, even if they seem at first to be far afield of your core business. You never know where a new idea might lead you, so have an open mind, be innovative, and always be on the lookout for new opportunities. Don't get complacent. Ask your customers what else you can do for them. And ask your vendors what your competitors are doing that you might be able to do as well. Keep up with new technologies, new markets, new ways of doing business. Don't just coast on your past success. Look to the future—or you won't have one.

Learn as much as you can about the financial side of your business. You have to know the basics of how your business is profitable—or you won't be profitable. Know your weaknesses, too. If this isn't your strength, hire the best person you can afford to complement you. Don't be cheap about it. Remember, you get what you pay for. Do what you do best, and hire the rest so your company will be strong on all fronts.

Buy a business if you can, then integrate it with other businesses you own, and build it up. Buy businesses that are similar to yours because you can make a profit on the business you buy simply when you consolidate overlapping operations. Don't merge, though. Buy outright whenever you can. Make sure you do extensive due diligence so you won't find any unpleasant surprises after you buy. And don't be afraid to walk away if you decide a business isn't right for you after all.

Always be open to selling your businesses. You don't have to sell, but it's always nice to have an offer. Watch what's happening in your industry, and if you think your industry is changing so dramatically that you may not have a business in the future, spread the word that you're open to offers. Choose when *you* want to sell, so that you're not forced to sell or go out of business.

Finally, work hard, look professional, and make sure you're generous to your key people so they don't look elsewhere. Good people are hard to find. Your reputation is everything. Don't squander it.

# ACKNOWLEDGMENTS

*I* WOULDN'T BE WHERE I AM TODAY WITHOUT THE support of my family: Nancy, my wife of fifty-two years who has stood behind me and played *the* major role in my success; my daughter Michele and her daughters Amanda and Melissa, and their father, Steven; my son Michael, his wife Elizabeth, and their children, Matthew and Caroline and Charlie; my parents and Nancy's parents; and my sister Andrea Berlent.

To my friends and colleagues Mark Claster, John Frisk, Barry Ginsberg, George Goldberg, Steven Goldman, Butch Johnson, Charles Kauffman, Debra Lafferty Jones, MaryLou Morgan, Mike Palmer, Glenn Popowitz, and Diana Scarpelli. This group played major roles as advisors and executives who made sure we created added value to our employees, our customers, and our suppliers.

# ABOUT THE AUTHOR

*H*OWARD L. BROWN GRADUATED FROM SYRACUSE University in 1967, got married to Nancy Goldis, and joined one of the family plastics companies (*The Graduate*). In 1972, he purchased Summit Office Supply, a $300,000 office-product company, which he expanded both through internal growth and acquisitions in the New York/New Jersey/Long Island/Westchester metropolitan area. In 1987, he sold Summit to Dutch company Buhrmann-Tetterode (BT) with company sales of $55 million. He remained with the company until 1996, increasing their footprint in the Northeast to more than $500 million. In September of 1998, Brown and investors purchased ten office-product companies in one day, including the main spoke, Allied Office Products in Hasbrouck Heights, NJ. Combined total sales of the companies were approximately $110 million. In 2006, the group of companies known as Allied Office Products was doing sales of $375 million, and Brown once again made an impressive sale—this time to Office Depot. In 2007 and 2008, Brown, his son, employees, and most of the same investors purchased Rentacrate, followed by Shred-X. His restricted covenant for the office-product industry ended in May of 2010 and HiTouch Business Services Inc. became the parent company of Rentacrate and Shred-X. In October of 2010, HiTouch Business Services, Inc. purchased My Office Products, Inc. (doing approximately $120 million in sales), giving HiTouch a nationwide distribution. His team successfully grew HiTouch as he had done with his previous companies, and in 2018, Brown again sold his company, this time to Staples. Along the way, his team introduced many firsts in the industry and developed the "one-solution sell."

Today, Howard enjoys spending time with all five of his grandchildren, playing golf, and giving back to the community. His family is actively involved in different charities, including CCFA (the Crohn's & Colitis Foundation of America) and many Jewish causes. His wife sits on the boards of and takes an active role in fundraising and leadership for these and other organizations.